Favorite Ways to
LEARN ECONOMICS

2nd Edition

Favorite Ways to
LEARN ECONOMICS
2nd Edition

DAVID A. ANDERSON

Centre College

JAMES C. CHASEY

Homewood-Flossmoor High School

THOMSON

SOUTH-WESTERN

Australia · Canada · Mexico · Singapore · Spain · United Kingdom · United States

THOMSON
★ ™
SOUTH-WESTERN

Favorite Ways to Learn Economics, 2e

David A. Anderson & James Chasey

VP/Editorial Director:
Jack W. Calhoun

VP/Editor-in-Chief:
Dave Shaut

Developmental Editor:
Jennifer E. Baker

Sr. Production Editor:
Elizabeth A. Shipp

Sr. Technology Project Manager:
Peggy Buskey

Sr. Marketing Manager:
John Carey

Sr. Manufacturing Coordinator:
Sandee Milewski

Editorial Production:
OffCenter Concept House

Art Director:
Michelle Kunkler

Cover Designer:
Joe Pagliaro Design

Cover Image:
© Getty Images, Inc.

Printer:
Globus Printing

Contents

Chapter 3 Consumer Choice 71

Chapter 4 Production Costs and Perfect Competition 87

Chapter 11 Aggregate Supply, Aggregate Demand, and Aggregate Expenditure   227

Classroom Experiments

Problem Sets

Chapter 12 International Economics   247

Classroom Experiments

Problem Sets

A Note to Students about Active Learning Experiments

Economics is the major of choice for rock stars like Mick Jagger, studs like Arnold Schwartzenegger, big shots like Sandra Day-O'Connor and George H.W. Bush, and billionaires like Ted Turner. For some, however, the appeal of this exciting discipline can be tempered by the challenge of grasping some of its fundamental concepts. We wanted to change that. The purpose of the active learning experiments in this book is to take you inside the box and show you how it feels to be an economic actor. That is, this book will lead you through activities that simulate production, sales, and various types of decision-making. Active learning has proven to be both popular and successful in eliciting the economic way of thinking and making concepts easier to learn and remember. These activities will help to clarify economic concepts, but only if you are an attentive, active, and engaged, participant. Be sure to take part earnestly and behave honestly. Passive participants will not reap the same educational rewards as those who jump in and become involved. Please read the introduction and scenario for each activity before class. After each activity, reflect on the experiment overnight and bring the completed worksheet to the next class meeting.

Above all, we hope that you enjoy this learning experience!

Best wishes,

Dave Anderson & Jim Chasey

About the Authors

David A. Anderson is the Paul G. Blazer Associate Professor of Economics at Centre College. He holds a Bachelor of Arts degree from the University of Michigan and Masters and Doctoral degrees from Duke University. Dr. Anderson has published research in the areas of active learning, classroom technology, and teacher evaluation, among topics from childbirth to the death penalty. He has received a National Endowment for the Humanities distinguished professorship, and grants for economic education projects from the 3M Foundation and the Andrew Mellon Foundation.

James C. Chasey received his Bachelor of Arts degree from Purdue University and his Master of Arts degree from the University of Illinois. As the Christa McAuliffe Fellow for Illinois, he received advanced training at the University of Chicago Graduate School of Business. Mr. Chasey has received the Freedoms Foundation Leavey Award, the Money Smart Award from the Federal Reserve Bank of Chicago, and the Purdue University outstanding education alumni award. He taught Advanced Placement Economics at Homewood-Flossmoor High School, and has served as Adjunct Professor of Economics at the College of DuPage and Governors State University.

Acknowledgments

The authors are grateful to the many who have contributed to this effort. Corey McCaffrey, Beth Stepanczuk, Cara Stepanczuk, Nate Olson, and Ashley Vinsel provided excellent assistance in preparing the manuscript. Hundreds of dedicated students field-tested the experiments and problem sets. Our families endured late hours and urgent deadlines. The faculty consultants at the AP Economics readings offered inspiration and support. The editors at South-Western provided valiant assistance and encouragement. Most importantly, we thank the students who have been willing to experiment with and puzzle over the fascinating field of economics, and the instructors who have given them the chance to do so.

Introduction to the Economic Way of Thinking 1

Classroom Experiment 1.A

Economics Is All Around Us: Hot Dog Vendors on the Beach

Time Required: *10 minutes*	**Level of Difficulty:** *low*
Materials: *none*	**Textbook Coverage of Underlying Topics:** *Arnold Ch. 1 , McConnell/Brue Ch. 1, Mankiw Ch. 1, Colander Ch. 1, McEachern Ch. 1, Baumol/Blinder Ch. 1*
Purpose: *To demonstrate that economics is everywhere and that optimal business strategies can be discovered with a small amount of economic reasoning.*	

Introduction

In the words of Nobel Laureate Paul Samuelson, economics can be "perfectly straightforward without being perfectly obvious." Optimal strategies aren't always obvious, but sometimes it's easier than you think to explain the behavior of business firms and make wiser decisions in your own endeavors with the help of a bit of economic reasoning. This experiment will put you into the shoes of an entrepreneur and ask you to make decisions about the three most important issues for new business owners: location, location, and location.

Scenario

The setting for this activity is a long beach with many hungry swimmers and sun worshipers. Imagine yourself as one of two hot dog vendors working this particular strip of beach. Whether or not you are one of the students asked to demonstrate your decisions on the simulated beach in your classroom, think carefully about where you would locate your hot dog stand under the circumstances described below. The scenario unfolds this way:

- The two hot dog stands on this beach have identical prices, products, and overall appeal.

- Beachgoers will purchase from whichever hot dog stand is *closest* to them.

- Beachgoers are evenly distributed along the beach.

- Only one hot dog vendor can move at a time.

In the classroom experiment, two representative hot dog vendors will be asked to station themselves on the beach and then take turns changing their location (if desired) in response to the other's location. The goal for each is to maximize hot dog sales.[1] Note that the shoreline along which the vendors may locate is a line from one side of the classroom to the other. There is no depth to the beach, meaning that they can move to the left or right along the beach, but they cannot venture forward into the dunes or backward into the water.

Reflections

(Please answer these questions **after** completing the classroom experiment.)

1. Describe the optimal strategy for choosing a location under the conditions described above.

2. In what situations do you see a similar strategy practiced near where you live?

3. What evidence of this strategy have you seen on a national scale?

---

[1]Assume that maximizing sales is the same as maximizing profits. This is true if the vendors can always sell another hot dog at a price that exceeds the cost of providing another hot dog. If the cost of selling another hot dog—the "marginal cost"—increases as more are sold, the vendors will only sell hot dogs as long as their additional revenue from selling one more exceeds the marginal cost.

4. Can you think of applications of this strategy that go beyond retail sales?

Afterthoughts

Believe it or not, you have just reasoned through some implications of spatial competition models described in the writings of economist Harold Hotelling. Although they are not immediately obvious, these findings and their retail applications make good sense after thought and experimentation. That is one of the reasons to study economics—there are important lessons about maximizing profit and happiness that elude the casual observer. The economic way of thinking can guide us to sensible solutions to everyday dilemmas; that's one of the things that makes economics valuable and exciting! We hope you agree.

Classroom Experiment 1.B

Production Possibilities Frontier Experiment: Links and Smiles

---

Time Required: *25 minutes*

Materials for Each Student:
2 sheets of 8 1/2 × 11 paper
1 roll tape
1 pair scissors
1 pencil or pen

Purpose: *After deriving your own production possibility frontier, you will better understand (and remember) what it's all about and the reasons for its shape.*

Level of Difficulty: *low (with high returns)*

Textbook Coverage of Underlying Topics:
Arnold Ch. 2,
McConnell/Brue Ch. 2,
Mankiw Ch. 2, Colander Ch. 2,
McEachern Ch. 2,
Baumol/Blinder Ch. 2

Introduction

A production possibilities frontier (also known as a production possibility curve) indicates all of the possible combinations of two goods that can be produced in one period using all available resources. By looking at a PPF, the trained eye can determine the opportunity cost of each of the goods at every level of production and whether or not production occurs at an efficient level. This experiment allows participants to derive and demystify production possibilities frontiers. After experimenting with different production goals, you will gain an understanding of input specialization and increasing opportunity costs.

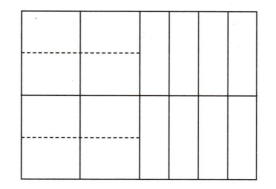

Setup

There are two paper inputs used in this experiment: 5 1/2" × 1 1/16" strips, and 2 3/4" × 1 1/8" rectangles. To obtain enough of each paper input for the whole experiment, you will need two 8 1/2" × 11" sheets of paper. Stack the two sheets on top of each other and make the following folds:

1. Fold the two most-distant ends together.

2. Fold the new most-distant ends together.

3. Undo the last fold and fold each of the most-distant ends in so that they touch the center line.

4. Without doing any unfolding, fold *one* side in once more so that it touches the center line.

5. Unfold the papers and you should have creases where there are solid lines in the illustration at the bottom of page 4. Cut along the creases, and cut the four wider strips in half as indicated by the dotted lines. You should then have 16 strips and 16 rectangles.

Scenario

In this experiment, every person represents a manufacturing firm. Firms will make "links" and "smiles."

A *link* is a 5 1/2" × 1 1/16" strip of paper wrapped into a circle and taped in place. Subsequent links are put through the previous link and taped to interconnect the links, forming a "paper chain," as are sometimes wrapped around Christmas trees.

A *smile* is manufactured by using scissors to round the four edges of a 2 3/4" × 1 1/8" rectangle and drawing two eyes and a smile on one side of the circle.

Although strips are best for making links, and rectangles are best for making smiles, creative cutting and taping will permit strips to be made into regulation smiles and rectangles to be made into regulation links. For example, a strip can be made into a rectangle by cutting it in half and taping the halves together, long edge to long edge.

Participants begin each round with four strips, four rectangles, a pen, a roll of tape, and a pair of scissors. Resources may not be carried over from one period to the next, and only one layer of paper may be cut at a time. Each round of production lasts 70 seconds. The production goals for each round are as follows:

Round 1: Make four smiles and as many links as you can.

Round 2: Make only links.

Round 3: Make only smiles.

Round 4: Make one smile and as many links as you can.

Record the number of links and smiles produced in each round.

	LINKS	SMILES
Round 1	_____	_____
Round 2	_____	_____
Round 3	_____	_____
Round 4	_____	_____

Reflections

(Please answer these questions *after* completing the classroom experiment.)

1. Draw your production possibilities frontier in the space below.

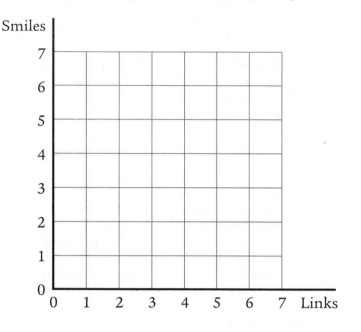

2. What was the opportunity cost of the first smile?

3. What was the opportunity cost of the last smile or two?

4. Why did the opportunity cost of making smiles increase as you made more of them?

5. In this experiment, you used strips that were specialized for making links and rectangles that were specialized for making smiles. Give two examples of real-world inputs that are specialized for the production of particular goods.

6. Explain how the use of specialized inputs results in a concave production possibilities frontier.

7. List two goods that are made from virtually identical (rather than specialized) inputs, and illustrate the general shape of a production possibilities frontier for those two goods.

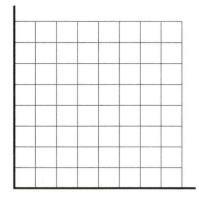

Afterthoughts

Having acted as producers and derived production possibilities frontiers, you should come away with a better understanding of the implications of specialized resources and increasing opportunity costs. In subsequent classes, you will be able to draw upon this experience to address issues of specialization and the role resources play in the shape of the PPF.

Problem Set 1.1

Allocating Resources

In the novel *Robinson Crusoe,* the main character is stranded on an island.

1. In general terms, how does the definition of economics relate to the challenges Robinson faces involving the resources available on his island? (If you don't know the definition of economics, make better friends with your textbook and your instructor!)

Assume that the following table lists the enjoyment that Robinson would receive from picking and eating raspberries.

Quantity of Raspberries	Level of Total Satisfaction in "Utils"
0	0
10	5
20	10
30	15
40	19
50	22
60	24
70	25
80	25

2. Robinson does not have to pay money for his fruit. Does that mean he gets a free lunch? If not, how would you measure the cost to Robinson of picking raspberries?

3. Assume that for Robinson the opportunity cost of the time it takes to pick each handful of 10 raspberries is 2 utils. How many raspberries should Robinson pick and eat?

4.   Are there situations in your own life in which you examine marginal costs and marginal benefits before making decisions? Elaborate.

Problem Set 1.2

Calculating Opportunity Cost

Workaholic Felix Alvarez is considering a trip to Sanibel Island, Florida for his spring vacation. He estimates that his roundtrip airfare would be $275.00, his car rental would cost $175.00, and his hotel expenses would $950.00 for his one-week trip. By going on vacation, Felix would not be able to work and would therefore not earn his usual $1,250.00 per week. Felix spends the same amount on food wherever he is. He always eats in restaurants, and his meals cost an average of $290.00 per week.

Calculate the "cost" of this vacation for Felix, and explain why you did or did not include each of the components described above in your calculation.

Problem Set 1.3

Marginal Analysis

Ada Okara has 9 hours available to study for her classes at Saint Aimee State University. The figures that follow are her best estimates of her performance on the upcoming exams in her classes.

HOURS OF STUDY	ECONOMICS	SPANISH	PSYCHOLOGY
0	20	30	35
1	39	51	53
2	56	65	69
3	71	77	79
4	82	86	87
5	86	91	92
6	88	95	95
7	89	97	97
8	90	98	98
9	91	99	99

Answer the following questions on the basis of the above information.

1. If Ada spends all of her time studying for Economics, what will her score be in Economics? Spanish? Psychology?

2. If Ada spends all of her time studying for Spanish, what will her score be in Spanish? Economics? Psychology?

3. If Ada spends all of her time studying for Psychology, what will her score be in Psychology? Spanish? Economics?

4. If Ada divides her time up evenly, studying 3 hours for each subject, what will her scores be in each of her classes?

5. How would you recommend that Ada allocate her time? Why?

Problem Set 1.4

Production Possibility Curves

Table 1 lists the various combinations of good X and good Y that can be produced. Use the information in Table 1 to answer questions 1–5.

1. Plot the following combinations of good X and good Y on Figure 1. Plot all points and connect them with a smooth curve.

Table 1	
make cookies	
GOOD X	**GOOD Y**
37	0
34	10
30	17
28	20
20	29
10	36
0	40

Figure 1

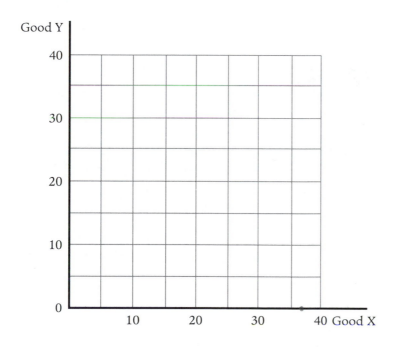

2. Calculate the cost of increasing production of good X from 0 to 10 units, as measured in the amount of good Y that would need to be sacrificed.

3. Calculate the cost of increasing production of good X from 10 to 20 units, as measured in the amount of good Y that would need to be sacrificed.

4. Calculate the cost of increasing production of good X from 20 to 30 units, as measured in the amount of good Y that would need to be sacrificed.

5. What happens to the opportunity cost as the production of good X increases?

6. Plot the following combinations of good X and good Y on Figure 2. Plot all points and connect them with a straight line.

GOOD X	GOOD Y
37	0
28	10
20	18
18	20
10	29
9	30
0	40

Figure 2

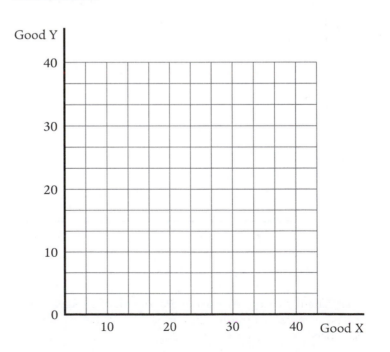

7. Calculate the cost of increasing production of good X from 0 to 10 units, as measured in the amount of good Y that would need to be sacrificed.

8. Calculate the cost of increasing production of good X from 10 to 20 units, as measured in the amount of good Y that would need to be sacrificed.

9. Calculate the cost of increasing production of good X from 20 to 30 units, as measured in the amount of good Y that would need to be sacrificed.

10. What happens to the opportunity cost as the production of good X increases?

11. A production possibility curve with a shape like the one in Figure 1 would be appropriately shaped if good X and good Y were what kinds of goods?

12. A production possibility curve with a shape like the one in Figure 2 would be appropriately shaped if good X and good Y were what kinds of goods?

Problem Set 1.5

Shifting Production Possibility Curves

Using the given production possibility curve as a starting point, show the result of each of the following.

1. An increase in population.

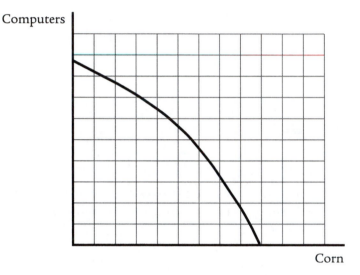

2. An improvement in technology applicable to corn production only.

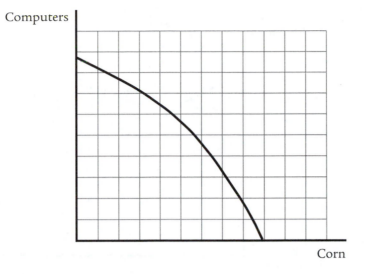

3. Increased literacy levels for all workers.

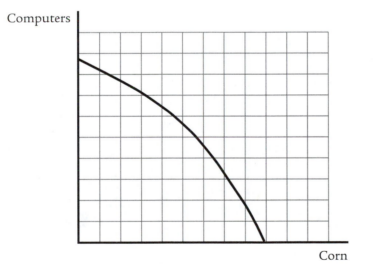

4. The depletion of nonrenewable resources used in the production of both goods.

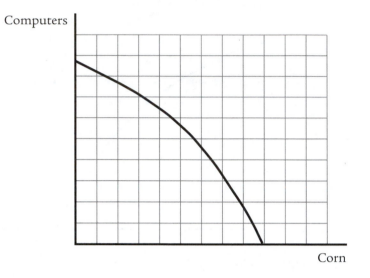

5. Increased consumer demand for computers.

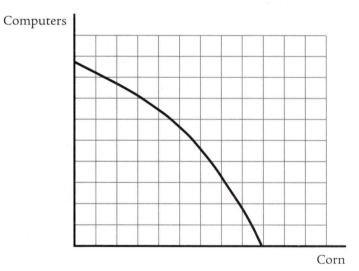

6. A lower cost of resources used to manufacture computers.

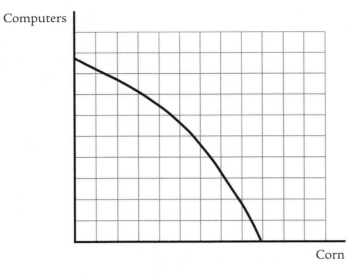

Problem Set 1.6

Three Economic Systems

1. There are three types of economic systems that can provide solutions to the central economic problem of scarcity (in addition to "mixed systems," which are combinations of the others). List those three sources of solutions.

   Indicate and explain which of the three types of systems would be best-suited for the following:

2. To achieve allocative efficiency.

3. To organize production so as to achieve a predetermined societal goal.

4. To organize production in a way that is easy to understand and reduces the possibility of job-related stress.

5. To organize production so as to correct for positive or negative externalities.

6. To organize production in a way that eliminates the need for centralized decision making and relies on the pursuit of self-interest.

7. Give an example of each of these three types of systems at work in the United States today.

Problem Set 1.7

Marginal Utility Problem

Assume that Czar Xavier finds only three goods, A, B, and C, for sale in Xavierland. The utility levels gained from the consumption of these goods are shown in the following table. Calculate the marginal utility values and enter them in the table.

TOTAL QUANTITY	GOOD A MARGINAL UTILITY	GOOD A TOTAL UTILITY	GOOD B MARGINAL UTILITY	GOOD B TOTAL UTILITY	GOOD C MARGINAL UTILITY	GOOD C UTILITY
0	0	0	0	0	0	0
1	30	_____	10	_____	25	_____
2	55	_____	18	_____	45	_____
3	70	_____	25	_____	57	_____
4	83	_____	31	_____	67	_____
5	90	_____	36	_____	75	_____
6	95	_____	40	_____	82	_____
7	95	_____	43	_____	87	_____

Use the marginal-utility data for Goods A, B, and C obtained in the table above to calculate the marginal utility per dollar for Goods A, B, and C. The prices of Goods A, B, and C are $7, $1, and $10 respectively. Enter these values in the table below.

QUANTITY	GOOD A MARGINAL UTILITY PER DOLLAR	GOOD B MARGINAL UTILITY PER DOLLAR	GOOD C MARGINAL UTILITY PER DOLLAR
1	_____	_____	_____
2	_____	_____	_____
3	_____	_____	_____
4	_____	_____	_____
5	_____	_____	_____
6	_____	_____	_____
7	_____	_____	_____

1. If the Czar wanted to maximize his utility, why would he not buy only Good B, as it is the least expensive?

2. If the Czar wanted to maximize his utility, why would he not buy only Good A, as it yields the highest total utility?

3. How would the Czar correctly determine the utility-maximizing amounts of Goods A, B, and C to purchase?

4. What would be the optimal amounts of Goods A, B, and C to purchase if the Czar had $48 to spend?

Supply, Demand, and Efficiency 2

Classroom Experiment 2.A

Buying and Selling Snipes in the Pit Market

Time Required: *25–30 minutes*	**Level of Difficulty:** *low to moderate*
Materials Required: *recording sheets (provided below) and valuation cards*	**Textbook Coverage of Underlying Topics:** *Arnold Ch. 4,*
Purpose: *To demonstrate the inner workings of a market and convergence to a market price.*	*McConnell/Brue Ch. 4, Mankiw Ch. 4, Colander Chs. 4 and 5, McEachern Ch. 3, Baumol/Blinder Ch. 3*

Introduction

You have probably read in your textbook about how supply and demand curves are derived and what they represent in terms of marginal benefits to consumers and marginal costs to suppliers. In this exercise, you will take part in the convergence of market forces that establishes quantities and prices to clear the market. This activity can be confusing to those who do not study the instructions, so please read the following carefully prior to the experiment.

Scenario

You will be assigned a role as either a buyer or a seller in what is called a *double-oral auction*. This name comes from the practice of buyers and sellers calling out their offers and demands such that all market participants can hear them. There are several versions of this experiment in the literature, some of which have no named product. Although the product you are buying or selling won't be tangible or change hands, we decided to name it a "snipe" to avoid the perplexing sale of nothing in particular.

Your instructor will give you a card indicating whether you are a buyer or a seller.

Buyers. If you are a buyer, the card you receive will also hold a number, which is the most you are willing to pay for a snipe. In other words, this is what a snipe is worth to you. If you can buy it for less than that amount, great. You have earned "consumer surplus"—a sort of bonus to buyers that equals the most they are willing to pay minus what they actually pay. You are not to pay more than the value on your card for a snipe. There is no reason to pay more for a snipe than what it is worth to you!

For example, if your card says $1000 and you manage to buy a snipe for $600, you get $1000 – $600 = $400 worth of consumer surplus. You would rather pay any price less than $1000 than not buy a snipe at all. You would be indifferent between paying $1000 and not buying a snipe (because you would be paying exactly what it is worth to you), and you would not be willing to pay $1001 or anything more than $1000 for a snipe. *Note: The prices used in these examples differ entirely from those used in the actual experiment in order to prevent price expectations based on these illustrations.*

Sellers. If you are a seller, the card will tell you the cost of "producing" a snipe. Snipes are raised to order, meaning that if you don't sell one, you don't need to raise one and you incur no costs. Thus, you will not sell a snipe for less than your cost of production. Your goal is to maximize your profit by selling a single snipe for as much above the production cost as possible. If you make a sale, your profit or "producer surplus" is calculated as the selling price minus your cost of production.

As an example, if your card indicates a production cost of $1000 and you manage to sell a snipe for $1500, your profit is $1500 – $1000 = $500. You would rather accept any price above $1000 than not sell a snipe at all. You are indifferent between selling for $1000 and not selling at all, because your profit at that price is zero. You would not be willing to sell your snipe for $999 or any other price below $1000.

The Workings of the Market. Your instructor will announce the beginning and ending of each trading period. You may only communicate with others about transactions during a trading period. When the period begins, buyers will shout out bids and sellers will shout out asking prices or "asks." Your voice is your only form of advertising in this market, so don't be timid. Remember that the amount on your card is your trading price at last resort—your intent is to transact at a price that is more favorable to you than the number on your card.

If you hear a price you would like to accept, or someone else accepts the price you are calling out, a transaction is born. As you are negotiating, take note of the prices from previous transactions that are posted on the chalkboard. They hold information about the spirit of the market. YOU MAY CARRY OUT AT MOST ONE TRANSACTION PER PERIOD. IF YOU MAKE A TRANSACTION BY BUYING OR SELLING A SNIPE, REPORT THE SELLING PRICE TO THE MARKET RECORD KEEPER (typically your instructor). AT THE END OF EACH MARKET PERIOD, WHETHER OR NOT YOU MAKE A TRANSACTION, RECORD THE RELEVANT INFORMATION ON YOUR SNIPE MARKET RECORDING SHEET. REMEMBER THAT EACH TRANSACTION PRICE MUST EXCEED OR EQUAL THE SELLER'S PRODUCTION COST AND FALL BELOW OR EQUAL THE BUYER'S VALUATION.

A Tax in the Snipe Market

(This is an optional variation on the above pit market experiment. The recording sheet, reflections, and afterthoughts below apply whether or not you have a round of taxes.)

Scenario

In the final period for the pit market game, a tax of $10 per snipe is imposed on the sellers of snipes. There is no tax on buyers. This means that while buyers will still pay up to the value on their card for a snipe, sellers cannot make a profit and therefore will not sell a snipe for less than $10 above their production cost. In a sense, taxes on sellers are part of the cost of bringing a product to market, so you can see this as increasing producers' costs by $10 per snipe. Thus, a seller with a card that reads $1000 will demand at least $1010 for the sale of a snipe. The other aspects of the market scenario are unchanged for this experiment with taxes.

SNIPE MARKET RECORDING SHEET

PERIOD	ROLE (CIRCLE ONE)	YOUR VALUE/ COST	CONSUMER/ TRANSACTION PRICE	AVERAGE PRODUCER SURPLUS	MARKET PRICE
1	buyer / seller				
2	buyer / seller				
3	buyer / seller				
4	buyer / seller				
5	buyer / seller				

(with tax)

Reflections

(Please answer these questions *after* completing the classroom experiment.)

1. What happened to the average market price over the first four periods? That is, did it wander randomly or was there an observable trend?

2. Compare your surpluses from the first and fourth transactions. How would you explain the changes in your behavior and your surplus?

3. In what ways was this experiment similar to real-world markets?

4. On the basis of the information your instructor revealed after the exercise about consumers' and producers' values and costs, construct the market supply and demand curves for the snipe market.

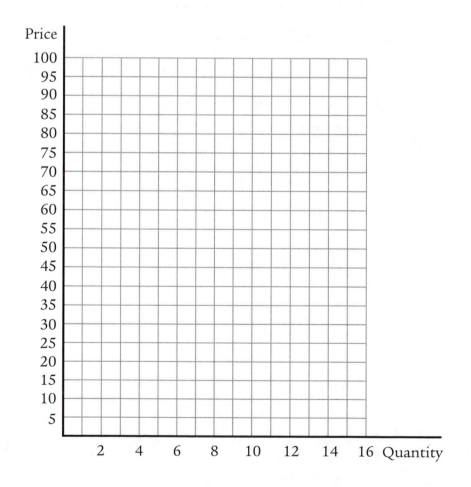

5. How did the average price in the final periods compare with the price that would maximize the sum of consumer surplus and producer surplus for all market participants—that is, the equilibrium price?

6. (Answer the remaining questions only if you included a tax in the last period.) How did the tax affect the average market price? Is that what you expected?

7. While the tax was imposed on the seller, did all of the burden fall on the sellers?

8. On the graph at the bottom of page 26, draw a new supply curve for sellers that reflects both the production cost and the tax cost. Does the new equilibrium price reflect what you observed in questions 6 and 7?

Afterthoughts

Adam Smith said that in a free market with participants acting selfishly, the outcomes would be efficient, as if guided by an invisible hand. Hopefully you got a taste of this efficiency by observing that the pit market in your class converged to an outcome close to the equilibrium that maximizes consumer and producer surpluses. With a tax, the incidence is theoretically independent of the party paying the tax. That is, buyers and sellers share the tax burden in the same way whether the tax is on the buyers or the sellers. In this experiment, it is likely that you saw the $10 per snipe burden of the tax shared between the parties, in that the average price paid by buyers increased by less than $10, and the amount kept by the seller (the average price minus the tax) decreased by less than $10. The sum of the additional payment by buyers and the decreased amount kept by sellers is the amount of the tax. If the sellers bore the whole burden of the tax imposed on them, the price for buyers would not change and the amount kept by sellers would decrease by $10. This would only happen if the demand curve was horizontal. Can you draw a graph and figure out why this is true?

Classroom Experiment 2.B

Penning Supply and Demand Curves

Time Required: *15 minutes*	**Level of Difficulty:** *low to moderate. Players make decisions under uncertainty.*
Materials Required: *Whatever pens or pencils you have on hand*	
Purpose: *To examine the influence of price on buying and selling decisions, and derive supply and demand curves along the way.*	**Textbook Coverage of Underlying Topics:** *Arnold Ch. 3, McConnell/Brue Ch. 3, Mankiw Ch. 4, Colander Ch. 4, McEachern Ch. 3, Baumol/Blinder Ch. 3*

Introduction

Supply and demand curves are central to economic analysis but far from intuitive upon first approach. We'd like to change that by having you reason through and form your own. In a way, you have supply and demand curves in your head for everything you could conceive of buying or selling. Of course, you may not have thought about them in the same way or with the same terminology that will be most useful in economics. Let's take a look at your present supply and demand "schedules"—a term used to describe either a table or a graph relating prices with quantities of a product supplied or demanded.

Scenario

When we refer to a "pen," let this mean a *working* (not broken) pen or mechanical pencil. (Wooden pencils are excluded.) You probably have a pen in your hand, a few in your backpack, and a few more in your dorm room or locker nearby. This activity will involve the actual buying and selling of pens, so think about what pens are worth to you. The first pen is necessary to take notes with. A few more are nice as back-ups or to provide variety. Additional pens might have value in the future as you lose pens or wish to store them in several locations. Alternatively, if the price is right, you might want to sell pens. Perhaps you have an overabundance, you know where to get them cheaply, or you need some spare change. You might be willing to sell one or two spare pens for very little, and more if the price warrants foregoing pens that are more important to you or are harder to obtain. *Note that you can only sell pens and spend money that you have on hand, so bring some of each to class.* There will be only one round of this activity with one selling price, so you do not need to worry about conserving money or pens for additional rounds.

With the given scenario in mind, complete the table. In the "I would buy" column, indicate the number of pens you would be willing to buy today in class with the money you have on hand at the prices listed. Be sure to write the total number for each price. For example, if you would buy 7 pens for 30 cents and 2 more if the price dropped to 20 cents, write "9" under "I would buy" at the 20 cents level. In the "I would sell" column, indicate the total number of pens you would be willing to sell at the different prices. *At each price you should have a zero either in the "buy" column or in the "sell" column,* because there is no sense in both buying and selling pens at the same price—that just makes for the effort of transactions with no gain. Leave the "market demand" and "market supply" columns empty for now.

PRICE (CENTS)	I WOULD BUY	I WOULD SELL	MARKET DEMAND	MARKET SUPPLY
140	_____	_____	_____	_____
130	_____	_____	_____	_____
120	_____	_____	_____	_____
110	_____	_____	_____	_____
100	_____	_____	_____	_____
90	_____	_____	_____	_____
80	_____	_____	_____	_____
70	_____	_____	_____	_____
60	_____	_____	_____	_____
50	_____	_____	_____	_____
40	_____	_____	_____	_____
30	_____	_____	_____	_____
20	_____	_____	_____	_____
10	_____	_____	_____	_____
0	_____	_____	_____	_____

In the diagram below, graph the numbers in your "buy" and "sell" columns.

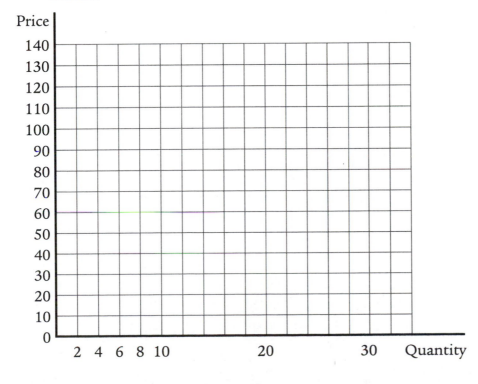

The graph of your "buy" quantities is your individual demand curve. The graph of the "sell" quantities is your individual supply curve. In class you will learn the quantities your classmates would buy and sell, and you can add up these quantities at each price to obtain the market demand and supply schedules.

Reflections

(Please answer these questions *after* completing the classroom experiment.)

For items 2–5, be sure to use the numbers on your graphs to answer the questions.

The following observations will come in handy when answering the questions below: Note that the table you filled in on page 29 indicates the values to you of each incremental pen. That is, when the quantity you would buy increases after the price falls, that means that the pens you would buy at the lower price, but not at the higher price, are worth the lower price but not the higher price to you. For example, if you would buy 3 pens for 40 cents each and 5 pens for 30 cents each, that means that the 4th and 5th pens are each worth roughly 30 cents to you, and certainly less than 40 cents since you didn't want to buy them for 40 cents. (We have simplified the scenario here by considering 10-cent jumps in price. One cent increments would have permitted a more precise estimate of valuations.) Similarly, when the quantity you would sell increases as the price goes up, that means that for the pens you would supply at the higher price and not at the lower price, the minimum you could be paid to supply them is roughly the higher price. Thus, if you would supply 4 pens at 80 cents each and 5 pens at 90 cents each, the minimum you could be paid to supply the 5th pen is roughly 90 cents.

1. Draw a graph similar to the one on page 29, but with a scale on the horizontal axis that accommodates the "market" demand and supply numbers for your class and graph the numbers.

2. What is the first pen worth to you? _____ What is the first pen worth to the person in your class who values it the most? _____

3. How many pens would you purchase if the market price were 20 cents each? _____ What are those pens worth to you? (Add the value of the 1st + value of 2nd + ...) _____ The difference between what you would pay for them ($0.20 × quantity) and their total value to you is called "consumer surplus." What would your consumer surplus be if the price of pens were 20 cents each? _____

4. How many pens would you supply for 90 cents each? _____ What is the smallest amount of money that you could be paid to supply that many pens? (Add up the minimum you would accept for the 1st + the minimum for the 2nd + ...) _____ The difference between the actual amount you would be paid ($0.90 × quantity) and the smallest amount you would accept for that quantity is called the "producer surplus." What would your producer surplus be if the price per pen were $0.90? _____

5. On the graph below, draw a replica of your individual demand curve from above. Label it "D." Think about how this curve would be different if you just won $1000 in the lottery or, alternatively, if you decided to take notes using a laptop instead. (If you're not sure of the general changes in your demand curve, try filling out another table like the one above given the new scenarios.) Draw your demand curve with increased wealth and label it "D_1." Draw your post-laptop demand curve and label it "D_2."

6. On the graph below, draw a replica of your individual supply curve from above. Label it "S." Think about how this curve would be different if you knew where to buy new pens for 10 cents each, or alternatively, if a 20-cent-per-pen-sold tax were imposed. Draw your supply curve with the 10-cent source and label it "S_1." Draw your post-tax supply curve and label it "S_2."

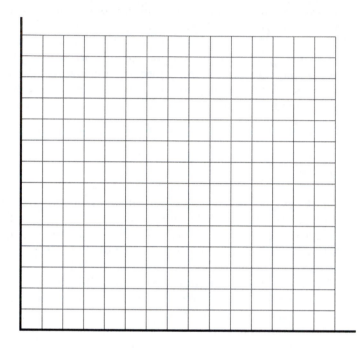

7. Beyond the changes described above,

    a. What else would shift your demand curve to the right, meaning that you would buy more pens at any given price?

    b. What else would shift your demand curve to the left, meaning that you would buy fewer pens at any given price?

    c. What else would shift your supply curve to the right, meaning that you would supply more at any given price?

d. What else would shift your supply curve to the left, meaning that you would supply fewer at any given price?

Afterthoughts

In some markets including the money market and the labor market, the same market participant can choose to be either a buyer or a seller, depending on where the price lies (the price of money being the interest rate and the price of labor being the wage rate). At low wage rates, you might hire someone else to mow your lawn, while at high wage rates you might knock on doors offering to mow other people's lawns. If the interest rate were 1 percent, you might decide to take out a loan to buy a car, whereas double-digit interest rates might bring you to put more money in the bank to be loaned out to others. In general, shifts in the market demand curve result from changes that affect people's willingness to pay for a good, such as advertising and income and the number of consumers in the market. Shifts in the supply curve result from changes in the cost of producing the good or in the number of suppliers.

Problem Set 2.1

Graphing Supply and Demand

The supply and demand schedules for Econ Videos in Econville are as follows:

PRICE PER ECON VIDEO	QUANTITY OF ECON VIDEOS DEMANDED	QUANTITY OF ECON VIDEOS SUPPLIED	SHORTAGE OR SURPLUS
$20.00	500	100	_____
$30.00	400	200	_____
$40.00	300	300	_____
$50.00	200	400	_____
$60.00	100	500	_____

1. Graph the demand for Econ Videos.

2. Graph the supply of Econ Videos.

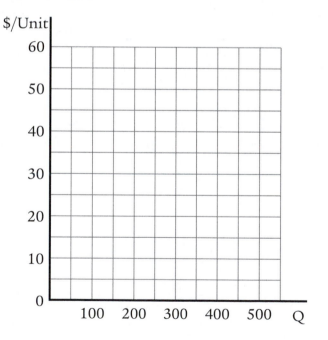

3. What is the equilibrium price of Econ Videos?

4. What is the equilibrium quantity of Econ Videos?

5. Fill in the Surplus or Shortage column.

6. What would result if the government of Econville set the price at $25.00?

7. What happens to price when a shortage exists in a market?

8. What happens to price when buyers' incomes increase? Assume the good in question is a normal good.

9. What happens to price when buyers' incomes rise? Assume the good in question is an inferior good.

10. Do you think equilibrium or disequilibrium prices are most common in the "real world"? Why?

Problem Set 2.2

Shifting Demand Curves

On the graph provided, use a dotted line to illustrate the influence on demand (if any) of the stated change.

1. A new, less expensive substitute good is introduced into the market.

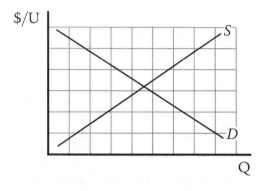

2. A law is passed that raises the age at which it is legal to consume this product.

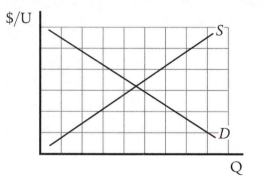

3. The price of a complementary good falls.

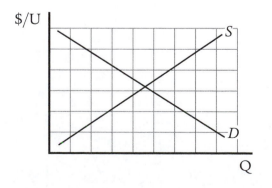

4. The government opens up its borders to completely free immigration.

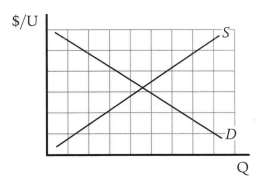

5. The good in question becomes more popular with consumers.

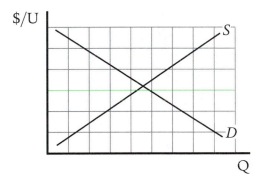

6. The cost of producing the good rises.

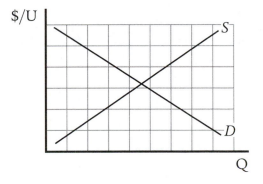

7. There is an expectation of higher future prices. (What would happen to present demand?)

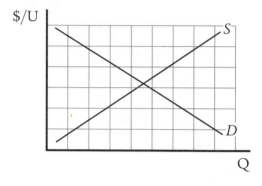

8. It is a normal good and buyers' incomes increase.

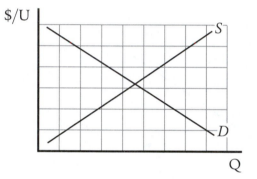

9. It is an inferior good and buyers' incomes rise.

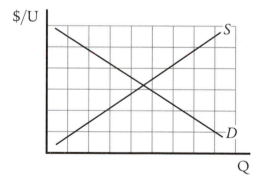

10. The price of the good rises.

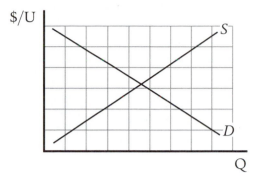

11. A change in technology makes production more efficient.

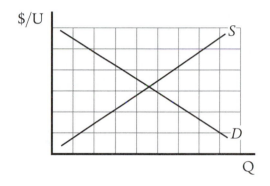

12. The price of an independent good rises.

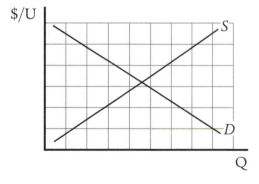

13. Create four problems like the preceding ones. Each should involve a change in a non-price determinant of demand that would shift the demand curve.

Problem Set 2.3

Shifting Supply Curves

On the graphs provided, use a dotted line to illustrate the influence on the supply curve (if any) of the given changes.

1. Advances in technology make production less expensive.

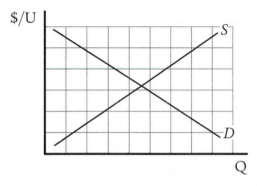

2. The resources formerly used to produce this product are banned.

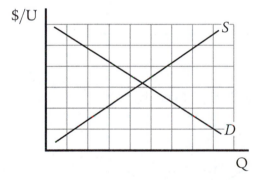

3. There is an increase in the selling price of another product that the same manufacturer can make instead of this product.

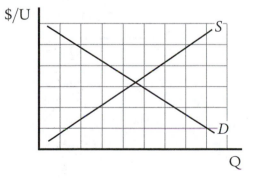

4. The selling price of this product increases.

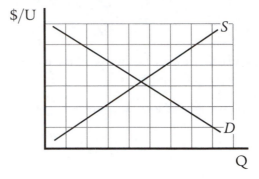

5. The good in question falls out of favor with consumers.

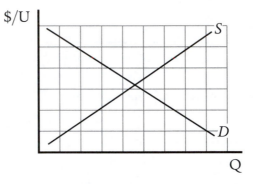

6. The cost of producing this product rises.

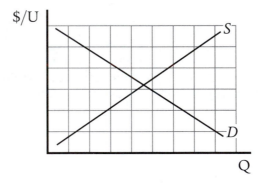

7.   Producers expect higher future prices.

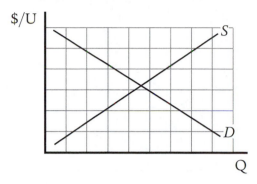

8.   The government decides to subsidize the production of this good.

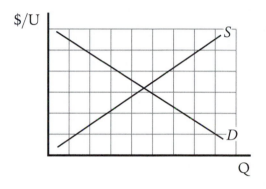

9.   It is a normal good and buyers' incomes rise.

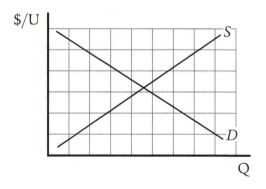

10. Foreign producers are now allowed to compete with domestic producers.

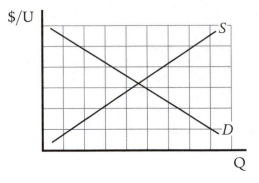

11. Create four problems like the preceding ones. Each should involve a change in a non-price determinant of supply that would shift the supply curve.

Problem Set 2.4

Elasticity

1. Calculate the total revenue at each price. Then use the Total Revenue Method (look at the change in total revenue as price changes) to categorize the price elasticity of demand as either elastic or inelastic in the range from the stated price to the price $10 higher.

PRICE	QUANTITY	TOTAL REVENUE	ELASTICITY
$100	1		
90	2		
80	4		
70	7		
60	11		
50	15		
40	18		
30	20		
20	21		
10	21		

2. Calculate the price elasticity of demand coefficient between each price and the price $10 higher using the "midpoint" or "arc" formula

$$\frac{(newQ - oldQ)}{averageQ} \div \frac{(newP - oldP)}{averageP}.$$

After calculating the coefficient, use your answer to categorize the price elasticity of demand as either elastic or inelastic in the price range stated.

PRICE	QUANTITY	COEFFICIENT	ELASTICITY
$100	1		
90	2		
80	4		
70	7		
60	11		
50	15		
40	18		
30	20		
20	21		
10	21		

Problem Set 2.5

Yuppie Scum Bumper Stickers

When Lucy Lugnut got out of prison, her husband Diesel decided that they would capitalize on her newly developed skills related to making license plates and go into the bumper sticker business. They decided to make a metal bumper sticker that buyers could bolt to their bumpers or hang from their gun racks. It said: "DIE YUPPIE SCUM."

They studied the market and found that if they charged

$1.00, they would sell 10,000

$1.50, they would sell 8,000

$2.00, they would sell 7,000

$2.50, they would sell 6,500

$3.00, they would sell 6,250

$3.50, they would sell 6,125

$4.00, they would sell 6,000

$4.50, they would sell 5,500

$5.00, they would sell 4,500

$5.50, they would sell 3,000

$6.00, they would sell 2

Lucy and Diesel initially put their bumper sticker on the market for $2.50. They can produce any quantity of bumper stickers at a unit cost of $0.50 each and decided to hire you as a consultant to advise them about pricing.

1. Calculate the total revenue earned at each of the prices listed above.

2. Indicate whether demand is elastic or inelastic for each 50-cent price range between the prices listed on page 47.

3. Would you advise them to raise the price to $3.00 even though they would sell fewer bumper stickers?

4. Would you advise them to lower the price to $2.00 in an effort to sell more?

5. Since Lucy and Diesel are the only providers of these bumper stickers, they can charge any price they choose. What price would you recommend? Why?

Problem Set 2.6

A Parking Lot Problem

WARNING: This problem set is not intended for the casual economics student. It contains material that may cause you to think! Be prepared to graph, analyze, calculate, and write short answers. User discretion is advised.

Once upon a time there was a school that let many students park their cars in its lot when they attended school. Then one day a big bad construction project was undertaken to add on to the school, and most student parking was eliminated.

Near the school there was a church that decided to help the students out of this predicament (and themselves to a few bucks.) The church figured that if they charged

$50/month, 1 student would park

$34/month, 2 students would park

$28/month, 3 students would park

$17/month, 7 students would park

$10/month, 11 students would park

$6/month, 14 students would park

$2/month, 19 students would park

$1/month, 25 students would park

1. Plot this information about the demand for parking spaces on the following graph. Label your line *D*.

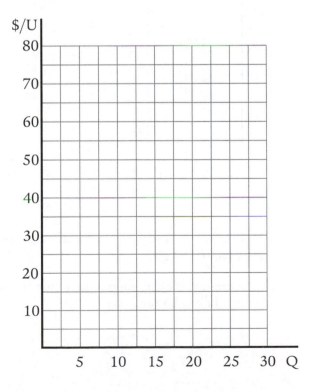

Now into our story comes the Wizard of Floz. In his infinite wisdom, he bans parking on all Village streets within a one-mile radius of the school (an option that students had enjoyed before the ban). There is much rejoicing at the church and many hallelujahs are being said because now if they charged

$75/month, 1 student would park

$58/month, 3 students would park

$46/month, 6 students would park

$36/month, 10 students would park

$25/month, 15 students would park

$18/month, 20 students would park

$12/month, 25 students would park

$10/month, 29 students would park

2. Plot this information on your graph and label it D_1.

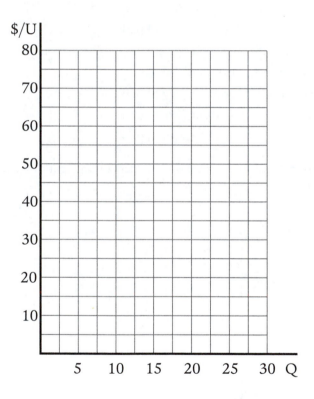

As the plot thickens, we further discover that the church has 15 available spaces each month.

3. Plot the unusual looking supply curve that results on your graph, and locate the equilibrium price.

4. Comment on the wisdom of a student petition to force the church to charge $10.00/month. What problem would arise? How could the church solve this problem without raising the price? Would you favor the proposed "price freeze" at $10/month? Why or why not?

5. To fill in the blanks that follow, calculate the total revenue for the church at each price and indicate whether demand is elastic or inelastic in the range between the prices.

   If the church lowered the price from $75 to $58, total revenue would go from _____ to _____

   so demand is _____

   $58 to $46, total revenue would go from _____ to _____

   so demand is _____

   $46 to $36, total revenue would go from _____ to _____

   so demand is _____

   $36 to $25, total revenue would go from _____ to _____

   so demand is _____

   $25 to $18, total revenue would go from _____ to _____

   so demand is _____

   $18 to $12, total revenue would go from _____ to _____

   so demand is _____

   $12 to $10, total revenue would go from _____ to _____

   so demand is _____

6. Why shouldn't the church charge the highest possible price ($75)?

7. What is appealing to the church about charging the equilibrium price?

8. Why would the economics students (perhaps not all of them, but certainly all of the really intelligent, hard working, cool economics students) like the church to charge the equilibrium price?

Who would not like the church to charge the equilibrium price?

What would be created if the price were set above the equilibrium price? (Use the term from economics.)

What would be the size of it?

What would be created if the price were set below the equilibrium price? (Use the term from economics.)

What would be the size of it?

Problem Set 2.7

Here Is a Message for Us

Sounding Board

Editor's Note: The following letter was submitted by Ardmoreita R.C. Lang who is a member of the public information council of the American Association of Petroleum Geologists.

Dear Editor:

Many years ago there was a western type town called Wildcat, Wyoming. This was a very prosperous town and everyone had all they needed. A tribe of Indians lived on the outskirts of town who were buffalo hunters and they kept the town supplied with meat.

The town's people always had plenty of meat to eat although they did not have much in storage. The town also got meat from other buffalo hunters who brought in buffalo from far away lands.

This made it very hard on the local tribe, as they only received $2.00 per buffalo and with the imported meat there was not much demand for local hunts. The town's people did not care too much for the Indians anyway and didn't want them coming into their town.

The town also had a Government agency that was supposed to help the townspeople and the Indians. But it seemed the Agency was always against the Indians. Although some leaders in the Agency were good to the Indians, like "Buffalo Hansen." Others like "Trader Jackson" sought to destroy the local tribe.

Then it happened! The far-away buffalo hunters got mad at the town and would not deliver any more buffalo meat to them. Panic hit the town as there was very little meat in storage and everyone would have to be rationed. The local tribe was at a loss, as they had no way to meet this sudden demand. The Indians were also rationed and had to wait in long lines and sometimes, after hours of waiting, find out they had run out of meat.

Most town people were not informed on what went on in this busy town and blamed the local Indian tribe for the shortage. (Some were so stupid they said the local tribe had purposely made unsuccessful hunts and had stampeded the buffalo over cliffs to create the shortage).

The Agency then came to the Indians and said, "We must have more Buffalo Per Day." (Now known as BPD.) "We must make our town independent, so we will not have to rely on far-away buffalo hunters anymore."

The Indians agreed. (As this was what they had tried to do all along). But they had many problems. The bows and arrows were old and had been stacked in a teepee for years. They would have to be repaired or replaced. New ones were ordered, but the bow and arrow makers had two years worth of back orders. Inexperienced braves would have to be recruited as many of the older braves had left when the buffalo hunts were slow and wages were low—never to return. The buffalo also were not as plentiful as before and the hunters would have to travel longer distances, into deeper canyons, at more expense. The bows and arrows would cost more money and they would have to pay higher wages to the braves. The price of buffalo would have to be raised to $10.00 each to cover the expense of the hunt. Some of the townspeople cried, "Excessive Profits." The buffalo hunts were carried on at a fast pace. The Indians worked very hard.

Many moons before the crisis, the Agency had set it up so that the Tribe had to give them part of their buffalo earnings each year. But the Tribe returned from many, many hunts without even the smell of a buffalo. The Agency would then return a small amount of their earnings so they could invest it in other buffalo hunts. This was called a "Depletion Allowance." Most of this had already been taken away from the Tribe. This was another reason the Tribe had slowed investments in the hunts.

Although the Indians worked hard, the townspeople still complained. They said the hunters' horses messed up their land and smelled up the air, even though most of them had never been to the hunting grounds. They complained that the wagons that hauled the buffalo meat and the hunting gear should not be allowed on the main road, even though the Tribe paid the town for road permits and road use tax.

Some of the Indians started hunting from the water in canoes. This was a great expense to the Tribe but they felt this might increase the supply of buffalo. The townspeople cried that the Indians would ruin the rivers. Although the Tribe took every precaution, one buffalo did fall into the water. The Indian who had shot the buffalo cleaned up the mess by himself and paid all the expenses while the townspeople stood on the bank and complained. The Indian was required to take his canoe and leave town. All the buffalo that were taken from water hunting have been forgotten, but the "Buffalo Splash Story" is still talked about today.

The Agency formed a committee and sent them to the Indian village. They told the Tribe that this group would make their hunting safer. They would put saddles on the horses, tie the braves to them, put safety tips over arrow heads and give them hard-toed moccasins to wear. (All at the expense of the Indian Tribe).

The Indians protested that this would greatly hamper the buffalo hunt and that the Tribe already had safety regulations. Why they even had their own safety council and safety braves checked every hunting party. But the Indians' argument fell on deaf ears and the new group stayed in command. The group was formed by townspeople consisting of store-keepers, bartenders, blacksmiths, and so on, none of whom had ever been near a buffalo hunt. The new group was called "Safety & Health for Indian Tribes."

Although the hunts became more and more expensive, it looked as if the Tribe might find enough buffalo for everyone to eat and maybe they could store some for the long, cold winters. Then an evil spirit came upon the Tribe. It was a leader from the Agency, good old "Trader Jackson." He said the depletion allowance should be taken away from the Tribe and the price should be rolled back to $2.00 per buffalo. The Agency and the townspeople agreed and it was done.

The beaten Indian Tribe put away their bows and arrows and returned to the reservation, never to hunt buffalo again. The winter was bad and all the townspeople starved to death. The town of Wildcat perished.

Don McElreath

Signal Oilfield Service, Inc.,

Casper, Wyoming

Answer the following questions based on the story.

1. On the graph below, show the effect of the "far away tribe" cutting off its supply of buffalo meat.

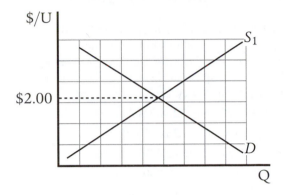

2. According to supply and demand analysis, what will happen to the price of buffalo meat when the far away tribe cuts off its supply?

3. If price were frozen at $2.00 per buffalo after the far away tribe cut off its supply, what would there be in the market for buffalo meat?

4. Show the effect of the Safety & Health for Indian Tribes act on the graph below.

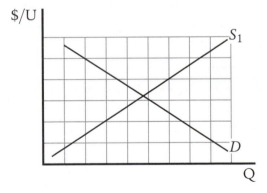

5. What tradeoffs must policymakers grapple with when deciding on safety regulations?

Problem Set 2.8

You Don't Have to Be Old to Be a Classic

Aging teen idol Ricky Rock decided to resurrect Woodstock. The only difference was that the event would be held in Illinois.

Headlining this psychedelic event would be Michelle Dinneen. Ricky and his sidekick Howard Spicer decided that if they held this event at the Galactic Music Theater in Pinley Tark and charged

$9.99, people would buy 32,000 tickets

$10.00, people would buy 28,000 tickets

$12.00, people would buy 23,000 tickets

$16.00, people would buy 19,000 tickets

$18.00, people would buy 17,000 tickets

$20.00, people would buy 15,000 tickets

$22.00, people would buy 13,000 tickets

$24.00, people would buy 11,000 tickets

$28.00, people would buy 7,000 tickets

$32.00, people would buy 5,000 tickets

1. Plot this information on the following graph.

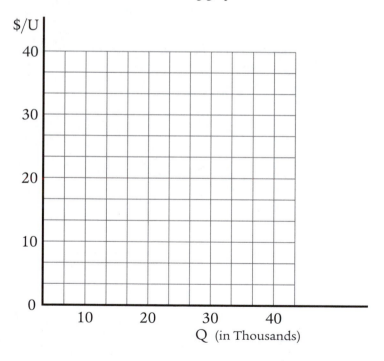

Rock promoter and TV personality Tamra Syrett went to the Galactic Music Theater to calculate costs. She figured that if she could get

$10.00 per ticket, she would offer 3,000 tickets for sale

$12.00 per ticket, she would offer 6,500 tickets for sale

$14.00 per ticket, she would offer 9,000 tickets for sale

$16.00 per ticket, she would offer 11,000 tickets for sale

$20.00 per ticket, she would offer 15,000 tickets for sale

$22.00 per ticket, she would offer 17,000 tickets for sale

$24.00 per ticket, she would offer 19,000 tickets for sale

$25.00 per ticket, she would offer 20,500 tickets for sale

$30.00 per ticket, she would offer 21,500 tickets for sale

$32.00 per ticket, she would offer 22,000 tickets for sale

$36.00 per ticket, she would offer 22,500 tickets for sale

2. Plot this information on the previous graph.

3. Identify the equilibrium price and quantity.

4. On the original graph, show what would happen if the "Ungrateful Alive" were added to the show and demand increased by 20 percent.

5. Demonstrate on the original graph what would happen if the traveling followers of the "Ungrateful Alive" (the Alive Feet) were rumored to be invading Pinley Tark to camp out and attend the concert. The local authorities would make Tamara Syrett pay those increased costs, and she would therefore lower supply by 15 percent.

6. Identify on the original graph the new equilibrium price that would result from the combination of 4 and 5 above.

7. On the original graph, indicate a nonequilibrium price that would create a shortage.

8. On the original graph, indicate a nonequilibrium price that would create a surplus.

Problem Set 2.9

Price Floor

The following graph shows a market in which the government has imposed a price floor. Answer the following questions based on the graph.

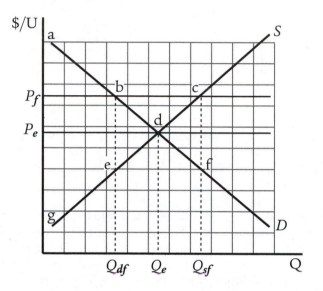

1. With this price floor in effect, what will happen to the actual price and quantity in the market and to the equilibrium (market clearing) price and quantity.

2. Comment on the efficiency of the equilibrium price and quantity that would prevail without the price floor in effect.

3. With the price floor in effect, what quantity would consumers want to purchase?

4. With the price floor in effect, what quantity would producers be willing to supply to the market?

5. With a price floor of P_f, what quantity would change hands and at what price?

6. What is the result of the quantity supplied being larger than the quantity demanded?

7. Using the letters on the graph, identify the efficiency (deadweight) loss due to the price floor. Hint: compare the total surplus (consumer surplus plus producer surplus) with and without the price floor.

Problem Set 2.10

Price Ceiling

The following graph shows a market in which the government has imposed a price ceiling. Answer the following questions based on the graph.

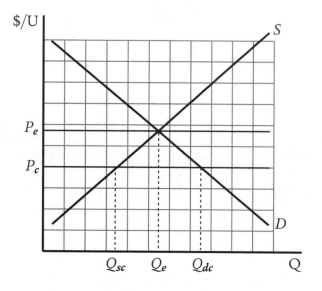

1. Interpret the effect of this price ceiling on the equilibrium (market clearing) price and quantity and on the actual price and quantity in the market.

2. Comment on the efficiency of the equilibrium price and quantity that would prevail without the price ceiling in effect.

3. With the price ceiling in effect, what quantity would consumers want to purchase?

4. With the price ceiling in effect, what quantity would producers be willing to supply to the market?

5. With a price ceiling of P_c, what quantity would change hands and at what price?

6. Describe the inefficiency associated with this price ceiling and show the "loss to society" on the graph below.

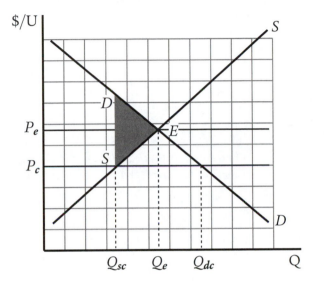

7. What is the economic term for the "loss to society" described in question 6?

Problem Set 2.11

Consumer and Producer Surplus

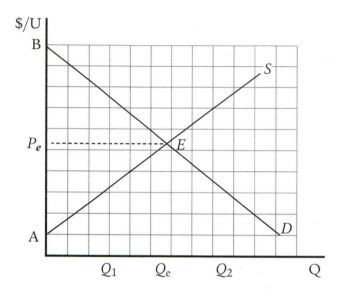

1. At equilibrium price P_e, the consumer surplus would be what area?

2. At equilibrium price P_e, the producer surplus would be what area?

3. When producing quantity Q_1, what is the cost to sellers of producing the last ($Q1$st) unit?

4. When buying quantity Q_1, what is the value to consumers of the last ($Q1$st) unit purchased?

5. Is Q_1 efficient? Explain why or why not.

6. When producing quantity Q_2, what is the cost to sellers of producing the last ($Q2$nd) unit?

7. When buying quantity Q_2, what is the value to consumers of the last ($Q2$nd) unit?

8. Is $Q2$ an efficient quantity to produce? Explain why or why not.

9. What unique efficiency property does Q_e possess?

Problem Set 2.12

The Cost of Taxation

Figure 1

1. Figure 1 shows the supply and demand for a product and the result-
    ing equilibrium price of P_e before the imposition of a tax. Figure 1
    also shows the result of imposing a tax that
    acts as a wedge between what buyers pay and
    what sellers receive for the product. The size of
    the tax is indicated on Figure 1. Show the price
    that buyers will now pay and the price that sell-
    ers will now receive. Show the quantity that will
    be sold with the tax in place.

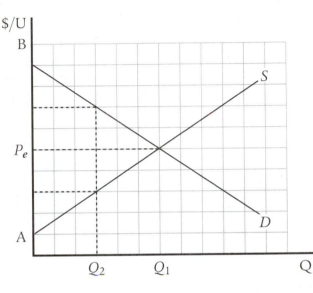

2. Show on the graph the amount of revenue gen-
    erated from the imposition of this tax.

Use Figure 2 to answer the following questions.

3. Identify by letters the size of the consumer sur-
    plus before the imposition of the tax.

Figure 2

4. Identify by letters the size of the producer sur-
    plus before the imposition of the tax.

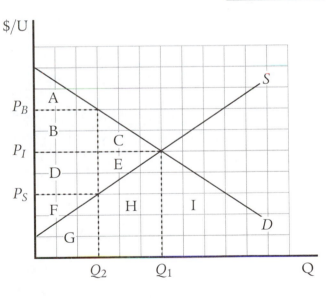

5. Identify by letters the size of the consumer sur-
    plus after the imposition of the tax.

6. Identify by letters the size of the producer sur-
    plus after the imposition of the tax.

7. Identify by letters the size of the revenue gener-
    ated by the imposition of the tax.

8. Identify by letters the reduction in consumer surplus after the impo-
    sition of the tax.

9. Identify by letters the reduction of the producer surplus after the imposition of the tax.

10. Compare the size of the tax revenue generated to the size of the loss in consumer and producer surplus.

11. Identify by letters the difference between the tax revenue gained and the total surplus lost. Where did that net loss go? What is the economic term for that loss?

Problem Set 2.13

Efficiency and Deadweight Loss

1. At price P_e shade in the consumer and producer surplus in the above graph, each in a different color.

2. Shade in the new consumer surplus that would result if the government established a legal price floor at P_f.

3. Shade in the new producer surplus that would result from the price floor P_f.

4. Compare the total size of the consumer and producer surplus that resulted from P_f to the total size of the consumer and producer surplus that resulted from P_e.

5. Identify the area on the graph that represents deadweight (or efficiency) loss.

6. Explain the source and meaning of this deadweight loss.

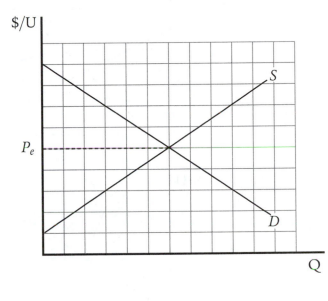

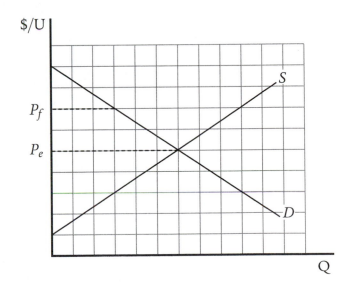

Problem Set 2.14

Elasticity and Deadweight Loss

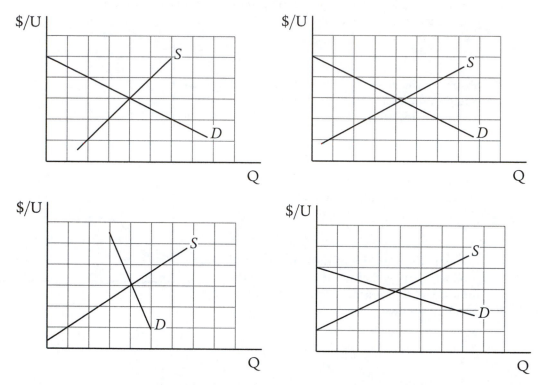

1. Suppose that a tax of equal size is imposed on each of the four markets represented by the provided graphs. On each of the four graphs, indicate and label the resulting wedge between what consumers pay and what producers receive.

2. On each of the graphs, shade in the size of the deadweight loss that would result from the imposition of the tax.

3. What can you conclude about the relationship between the elasticity of demand and the deadweight loss?

4. What can you conclude about the relationship between the elasticity of supply and deadweight loss?

Problem Set 2.15

Consumer Surplus

Assume that there are only six consumers in a small local market for root beer. These consumers are Gina, Milton, Pauline, Jim, David, and Joy. Each of these consumers has a distinctly different preference for root beer, and the utility they derive from its consumption is listed in the following table. The values in the table are the maximum amounts of money that each of these consumers of root beer would be willing to pay for a case of root beer.

CONSUMER	WILLINGNESS TO PAY
Gina	$75
Milton	$60
Pauline	$50
Jim	$45
David	$25
Joy	$10

Answer the following questions based on the information above.

1. How many cases of root beer would be sold for a price of $100?

2. How many cases of root beer would be sold for a price of $50?

3. How many cases of root beer would be sold for a price of $20?

4. Derive the market demand curve by creating a bar graph with a bar of width one and height equal to the willingness to pay for each consumer, in descending order, on the graph to the right.

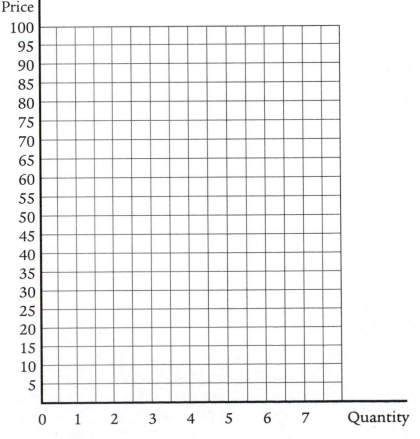

5. Shade in the consumer surplus that would accrue, and to whom, if the price of root beer were $45 per case.

6. What does consumer surplus measure?

Problem Set 2.16

Producer Surplus

In addition to being consumers of root beer, Gina, Milton, Pauline, Jim, David, and Joy are providers of economics lectures. Each of these lecturers places a value on their time and would be willing to provide these lectures for a price. The following table lists the minimum amounts each of them would be willing to accept for a one-hour economics lecture. Barring expenses for slides, travel, and the like, these marginal cost figures reflect the opportunity cost of the lecturers' time.

PRODUCER	MARGINAL COST
Gina	$1000
Milton	$900
Pauline	$700
Jim	$500
David	$300
Joy	$100

Answer the following questions based on the information above.

1. How many lectures would be given if the price of economics lectures were $50?

2. How many lectures would be given if the price of economics lectures were $500?

3. How many lectures would be given if the price of economics lectures were $900?

4. Derive the market supply curve by creating a bar graph with a bar of width one and height equal to the marginal cost for each producer, in ascending order, on the graph.

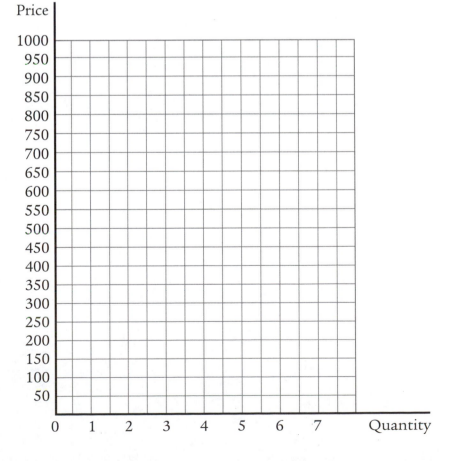

5. Shade in the producer surplus that would accrue, and to whom, if the price of economics lectures were $500 per lecture.

6. What exactly does producer surplus measure?

Consumer Choice

Classroom Experiment 3.A

Experimenting with Marginal Utility: Popcorn and Soda-Pop

Time Required: *20 minutes*	**Level of Difficulty:** *low*
Materials Required: *Popcorn, soda-pop, small cups, large sacks*	**Textbook Coverage of Underlying Topics:** *Arnold Ch. 19, McConnell/Brue Ch. 21, Mankiw Ch. 21, Colander Ch. 8, McEachern Ch. 6, Baumol/Blinder Ch. 4*
Purpose: *To demonstrate diminishing marginal utility and the virtues of balance*	

Introduction

The economic analysis of consumer choice involves graphs that make a lot of sense when properly understood, but without immersion in the process that generates them, their meaning seldom sticks in the heads of would-be economists. This experiment will give you a reference point for solid understanding. At issue is the satisfaction we obtain from increasing quantities of a particular good and the combinations of two goods that make us equally happy. Economists use the word "utility" to refer to satisfaction and often speak of units of satisfaction as "utils." Note that both the sources of utility and the levels of utility gained from particular goods differ from person to person. It is difficult to say in absolute terms that one person is happier than another person, and the units chosen to measure utility matter very little, but much of economic theory is based on the assumption that individuals make decisions in order to maximize their utility. It thus becomes meaningful to examine the characteristics of utility. Wet your lips and get ready to learn something important.

Scenario

Just to reassure you, at the end of this experiment, everyone will be able to enjoy some food and drink. Initially, three hungry subjects and three thirsty subjects will be selected for study. If you are not among them, observe their behavior and think about how you would respond in the same situation. In the interest of spontaneity, we will not explain any more of what is to come in this experiment, but your instructor will keep things hopping and popping.

Reflections

(Please answer these questions *after* completing the classroom experiment.)

1. Marginal utility is the name for the additional utility gained from one more unit of a good. What happened to the marginal utility of popcorn as the research subjects ate more and more? How would you explain this phenomenon?

2. Draw a graph of the marginal utility of the middle subject.

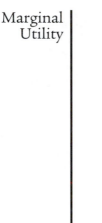

Marginal Utility

Handfuls of Popcorn

3. In the second round of this game, subjects were asked to reveal the largest number of handfuls of popcorn they would trade for a beverage. Which of the following is the wisest strategy to take in this situation?
    a. Trade at most the amount of popcorn that equals the number of cups of soda-pop you are receiving.
    b. Trade at most the amount of popcorn that gives you the same amount of utility as the beverage in question.
    c. Trade at most the amount of popcorn that you really have no desire for at all.
    d. Other: (write your own, if you desire).

Explain the virtues of your chosen strategy, whether a, b, c, or d.

4. If a subject traded exactly the amount of popcorn that gave him or her as much utility as the beverage received, what would this imply about the subject's total level of utility before and after making the trade?

5. Note that your instructor has drawn a pair of points on each of the graphs. For each pair, one point represents the subjects having only pop or popcorn, and the other represents the subjects having one unit of one of the goods and a reduction in the other good equal to the most they would trade for that one unit of the first good. Keeping your answers to questions 3 and 4 in mind, what can you say about the subjects' levels of utility at each of the two points in each pair?

6. On the basis of your own estimation, draw your demand curve for soda-pop and label it D_{me}. On the same graph, draw the demand curve for soda-pop that you would estimate for one of the popcorn eaters *after* the first round of this experiment and label it D_{ate}. (If you were one of the first round eaters, draw your demand curve and that for one of the non-eaters.) Explain the difference between these two curves.

Price ($)

Cups of Soda-Pop

Afterthoughts

If you answered questions 3–5 correctly, you might have a good idea why the lines your instructor drew on the graphs are called "indifference curves." If not, this will be explained during the debriefing. In the first round of this experiment, you saw diminishing marginal utility before your very eyes. Although it may have seemed fairly unrelated, the second round of the experiment demonstrates the same concept in another way. Starting with a lot of popcorn and no soda-pop, the marginal utility from the first cup is high and the marginal utility of one handful of popcorn is low because there is so much popcorn. Thus, the subject is willing to trade a lot of the less-valued popcorn for a little of the much-valued soda-pop. After some trades of popcorn for soda-pop have been made, *due to the diminishing marginal utility of soda-pop as more is obtained and the increasing marginal utility of popcorn as less is held*, the amount of popcorn that will be traded for another cup of soda-pop decreases. Think about how this explains the shape of indifference curves and our tendency to prefer balance in our holdings of two goods.

Classroom Experiment 3.B

Indifference Curve Experiment: Are You Sure?

Time Required: *30–40 minutes*

Materials Required: *colored sidewalk chalk—1–2 pieces per person*

Purpose: *To allow students to reason through the logic of indifference curves.*

Level of Difficulty: *high. Only advanced students figure it all out,*

but the experience of thinking it through and grappling with the mystery is beneficial to everyone.

Textbook Coverage of Underlying Topics:
*Arnold Ch. 19,
McConnell/Brue Ch. 21,
Mankiw Ch. 21, Colander Ch. 8,
McEachern Ch. 6,
Baumol/Blinder Ch. 4*

Introduction

Utility is another name for happiness, and utility theory is about what makes us happy. Indifference curves represent the combinations of two goods that give us the same level of happiness. For example, if you are equally happy with 2 slices of pizza and 10 cans of soda-pop per week as with 7 slices of pizza and 4 cans of soda-pop per week, the points (2 slices, 10 cans) and (7 slices, 4 cans) are on the same indifference curve. Both combinations give you the same level of utility (happiness)—say, 25 smiles or 37 "utils" or however you want to measure it.

In this experiment we will think about what indifference curves generally look like under the assumption that there is no "free disposal." That means you must consume everything you receive. Do you remember what food, if any, you left on your tray after lunch yesterday? That was an example of free disposal. You wanted some of those french fries but not all of them, and you were free to dispose of those you didn't want. When there is *no* free disposal, additional units of items that are initially good become bad after the point where you have all that you could possibly want. On a cold winter day, a first winter coat is greatly appreciated. One might wear a second coat if it were not too bulky, but one would probably pay money *not* to have to wear a third or fourth coat, or more. When one would be willing to give up money (or some good) in exchange for being able to wear *fewer* coats, coats have become a bad rather than a good. You may remember times when your parents enforced a no-free-disposal eating policy on you, which perhaps made carrots a bad after a few bites. If you could slip them to the dog under the table, you had free disposal, and carrots did not become a bad.

Scenario

Assume that you enjoy pizza and soda-pop in moderation and that you must eat every slice of pizza and drink every can of soda-pop that you receive within a period of a week. Suppose that you currently receive 5 cans of soda-pop and 1 slice of pizza per week. Your mission is to draw a line that goes through all of the other combinations of cans and slices per week that make you exactly as happy as you are with 5 cans and 1 pizza slice. In order to allow this line to be smooth, assume that partial cans and slices are also possibilities for consumption. Although this graph will be different for everyone due to subjective preferences, the general shape should be the same. Remember that this does not have anything to do with how much you can afford; it is only about how happy different combinations would make you. Your instructor will give you a few pieces of sidewalk chalk with which you can experiment drawing graphs on the sidewalk in front of your building. As you think through the shape of this beast, your instructor will come by periodically, pointing to sections of your graph that require more thought and asking, "*Are you sure* about this part?" If this seems difficult, relish the challenge. You wouldn't want to waste your time "learning" something that is obvious!

Hints:

1. For each item, think about the quantity beyond which it becomes a bad. As a good changes to a bad, what changes about the tradeoffs are necessary in making you equally happy?

2. Think about how many cans you would trade for a slice when you have many cans and just a few slices. How does this maximum voluntary tradeoff change as you get more and more slices and fewer and fewer cans?

Reflections

(Please answer these questions *after* completing the classroom experiment.)

1. What would be some real-life examples of goods that become bads because there is no "free disposal"?

2. Does money ever become a bad?

3. Draw a mini version of your indifference curve graph below.

4. What would this indifference curve look like with free disposal? Hint: That means the goods never become bads, because before they do, you could just dispose of them instead of having to consume them.

5. What would this indifference curve look like with no free disposal for pizza but free disposal for soda-pop?

Afterthoughts

The line you drew for reflection 4, if correct, is a standard indifference curve. Economists typically assume that the opportunity for free disposal exists, although there are certainly times when it does not. The indifference curve is a hard graph to fully comprehend, but now that you've puzzled over its structure for a while, you should have a more clear and lasting understanding of it. Cheers!

Problem Set 3.1

Budget Lines

1. Suppose that a consumer has an income of $10 per period and that he must spend it all on meat or potatoes. If meat is $1.00 per pound and potatoes are $.10 per pound, draw the consumer's budget line on the graph.

2. In the previous case, what would happen to the consumer's budget line if his income increased to $12 per period?

3. What would happen to the budget line in problem 2 if the price of meat increased to $2.00 per pound?

4. What would happen to the budget line in problem 3 if the price of potatoes increased to $.20 per pound?

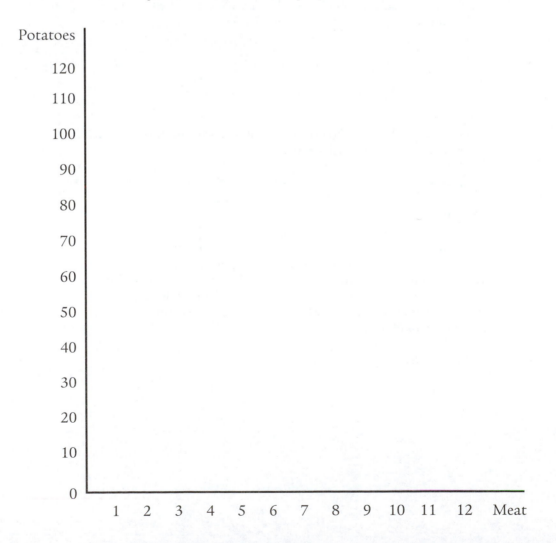

Problem Set 3.2

Indifference Curves

1. What are some of the important assumptions that economists make for the purpose of constructing indifference curves?

2. Draw the indifference curve that includes the following market baskets. Each of these market baskets gives the consumer an equal amount of satisfaction.

MARKET BASKET	MEAT (LBS)	POTATOES
1	1	8
2	2	5
3	4	3
4	7	2
5	9	1.5

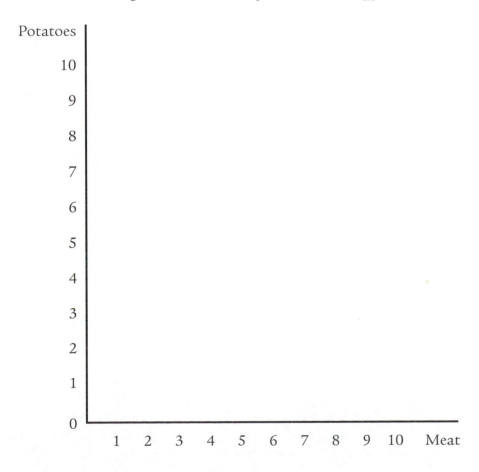

3.   Define utility.

4.   How does cardinal utility differ from ordinal utility?

5.   Which of these measures of utility are economists most concerned with today?

Problem Set 3.3

Budget Lines, Indifference Curves, and Consumer Satisfaction

1. Suppose that a consumer has an income of $10 per period and that he must spend it all on meat and potatoes. If meat is $1.00 per pound and potatoes are $1.00 per pound, draw the consumer's budget line on the graph.

2. Draw the appropriate changes that would result from the price of potatoes increasing to $2.00 per pound.

3. Draw the appropriate changes that would result from the price of meat increasing to $2.00 per pound, with the price of potatoes at $2.00 per pound.

4. Although you don't have information on the specific location of indifference curves for this consumer, draw several that obey the normal assumptions about indifference curves. Include in your drawing the three indifference curves that indicate the quantity of meat and potatoes that would be consumed with the budget lines defined in parts 1–3 of this problem set, and label these quantities on the axes of the graph as M_1 (the quantity of meat consumed with the budget line in part 1), M_2, M_3, P_1, P_2, and P_3.

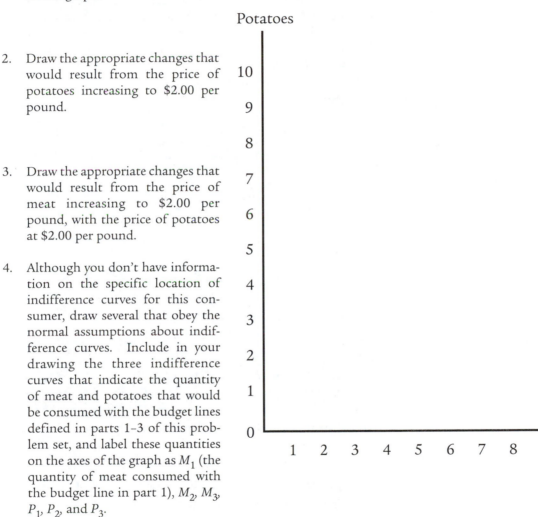

Problem Set 3.4

Utility Maximization

Suppose that through market research, economists have discovered that consumers in general express a fairly consistent set of preferences for products X and Y. Some economists have even been able to quantify these preferences. Thanks to the tireless efforts of two of the up-and-coming economists of our time and their unique ability to design and build a utility measuring machine, we have been able to obtain the following set of data. Levels of consumer satisfaction are measured in levels of Z. Since Z is an ordinal measurement, Zs are simply ordered, Z2 being a higher level of satisfaction than Z1. Z5 is a higher level of satisfaction than Z4 and so on. The following table shows levels of Z and the various combinations of X and Y that result in those levels of satisfaction being obtained.

Z1

X	28	24	21	17	13	8	3	2	1	$\frac{1}{2}$	$\frac{1}{4}$	$\frac{1}{8}$
Y	$\frac{1}{2}$	1	$1\frac{1}{2}$	$2\frac{1}{2}$	$3\frac{1}{2}$	5	7	$8\frac{1}{4}$	12	20	30	40

Z2

X	28	24	20	14	8	5	3	2	1	$\frac{1}{2}$	$\frac{1}{4}$
Y	$1\frac{1}{4}$	2	3	5	7	8	12	14	20	30	40

Z3

X	28	22	16	10	8	6	3	2	1	$\frac{3}{8}$
Y	$2\frac{1}{8}$	4	6	$8\frac{1}{4}$	9	12	20	24	30	40

Z4

X	28	20	14	10	8	6	4	2	1	$\frac{1}{2}$
Y	4	6	8	10	14	18	23	28	33	40

Z5

X	28	26	20	15	$12\frac{1}{2}$	12	8	7	6	4	2	1
Y	$5\frac{1}{2}$	6	8	10	$11\frac{1}{2}$	12	20	22	24	30	35	38

Fortunately for economics students, further information is available for products X and Y.

In year 1, the price of X is $1.00 and the price of Y is $ .66$\frac{2}{3}$.

In year 2, the price of X is $1.00 and the price of Y is $ .80.

In year 3, the price of X is $1.00 and the price of Y is $1.00.

In year 4, the price of X is $1.00 and the price of Y is 1.33\frac{1}{3}$.

In year 5, the price of X is $1.00 and the price of Y is 1.81\frac{8}{10}$.

In year 6, the price of X is $1.00 and the price of Y is 2.35\frac{3}{10}$.

Show on the following graph the various combinations of X and Y that consumers would obtain, assuming that they were rational and maximized their satisfaction every year with an income of $20. Connect the points representing these combinations to illustrate the price-consumption curve.

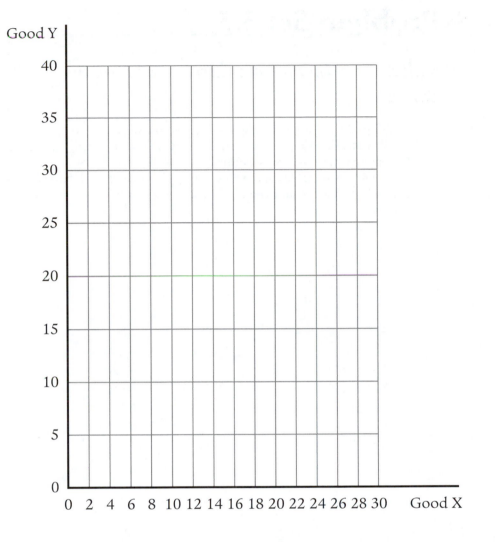

Problem Set 3.5

Budget Lines, Indifference Curves, and Demand Curves

In this problem, you will derive the demand for Yaks. Let Y represent the number of Yaks, X represent the number of Xats, and Za, Zb, Zc, Zd, and Ze represent various levels of utility.

The following table lists levels of satisfaction associated with various amounts of good X and good Y. The Zs represent levels of satisfaction, with Za > Zb > Zc > Zd > Ze.

Za

X	26	12	5	
Y	7.5	13	33	

Zb

X	26	11	4	
Y	5	11	30	

Zc

X	26	8	3	
Y	1.25	9	28	

Zd

X	26	5.5	2	
Y	.87	8.25	28	

Ze

X	26	13	1	.5
Y	.5	1	12	33

PRICES	X	Y
Year 1	$1.00	$1.00
Year 2	$1.00	$1.25
Year 3	$1.00	$1.85
Year 4	$1.00	$2.38
Year 5	$1.00	$12.50

1. Plot the indifference curves listed above and label them Za, Zb, Zc, Zd, and Ze on Figure 1.

2. Plot the budget lines for years 1 through 5 on Figure 1 with a budget of $25.00.

3. Locate the points of tangency between the indifference curves and the budget lines on Figure 1, connect them, and label this the Price Consumption Curve for Product Y.

4. Replot the Price Consumption Curve for Product Y on Figure 2 using price and quantity on the axes.

5. Calculate the price elasticity of demand from year 1 to year 2 and from year 4 to year 5. Calculate these elasticities using the "arc" or "midpoint refinement" formula:

$$\frac{(newQ - oldQ)}{\text{average } Q} \Big/ \frac{(newP - oldP)}{\text{average } P}.$$

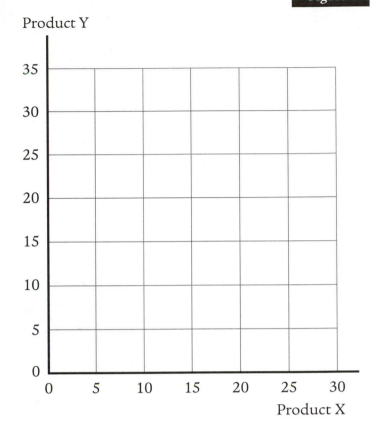

Figure 1

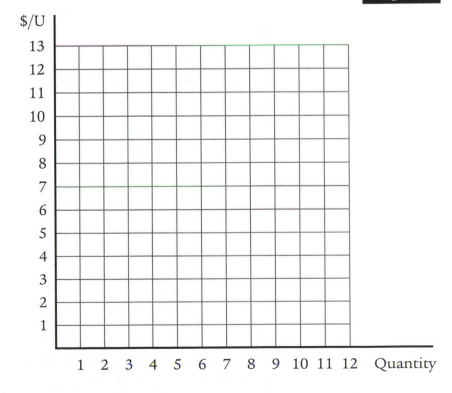

Figure 2

Production Costs and Perfect Competition 4

Classroom Experiment 4.A

Diminishing Marginal Product Experiment: The Econville Link Factory

Time Required: *20–30 minutes*	**Level of Difficulty**: *low to moderate.*
Materials Required: *Stack of 81/2" × 11" paper (can have been used previously—recycle!)* *Two or three tape dispensers with tape* *Two or three pairs of scissors* *Two or three student desks*	**Textbook Coverage of Underlying Topics:** *Arnold Ch. 21, McConnell/Brue Ch. 22, Mankiw Ch. 13, Colander Ch. 9, McEachern Ch. 7, Baumol/Blinder Ch. 6*
Purpose: *To demonstrate the reality of diminishing marginal product and provide data with which to calculate cost curves.*	

Introduction

When a car gets stuck in the snow or someone gets hurt in an accident or there's a new train set to be put together, the first few people who provide assistance do a lot of good. As more people join the effort and try to help out, their contributions become less and less valuable. When Uncle Charlie enters the room as the tenth person trying to put the train track together, he's more disruptive than helpful. There's a lesson to be learned here about manufacturing. As you might have anticipated, you're about to experience it first-hand.

Scenario

In this experiment, two or three factories within the classroom will produce *links*. You may remember this product from the *links and smiles* experiment. A link is a strip of paper approximately 5 1/2" × 1 1/4" cut from an 8 1/2" × 11" sheet. The strip is then wrapped into a circle and taped to form a ring. The next strip is cut, placed *through the previously made ring*, and taped to interconnect the two paper rings to form the beginnings of a "paper chain." The process is repeated for as many links as you can produce within the given time.

Production in the link factories proceeds as follows:

1. Each of the two or three factories gets one desk to work with. Your instructor will set these desks up in the front of the room with one stack of paper (ten sheets is enough), one pair of scissors, and one tape dispenser on each desk.

2. Each factory begins with a single production worker.

3. Production periods last 45 seconds, beginning and ending with a signal from your foreman/instructor.

4. After each production period, the employees at each plant count the number of *completed and linked* links made and report this number to the foreman for record keeping on the board. The foreman reserves the right to inspect each of the chains to assure quality control.

5. Before starting each successive production period, all bits of tape, paper strips, and partially made links are discarded, and one additional worker (but no more tape dispensers, scissors, or desks) is added to each factory. *Note that the workers are the variable input in this production process, and the scissors, tape, paper, and desks are the fixed inputs.*

Steps 3 through 5 will be repeated for a total of five or more production periods, with one new worker added to each factory each period.

Record the total output produced with each number of workers for use in the Reflections below.

Reflections

(Please complete this section *after* completing the experiment above.)

Your factories may or may not have produced results that would be considered typical. The following figures show what might happen in a typical links factory.

> 1 worker produced 2 links
>
> 2 workers produced 6 links
>
> 3 workers produced 8 links
>
> 4 workers produced 9 links
>
> 5 workers produced 9 links

1. Complete the following table based on production in your plant. If you did not work in a plant, you may base your answers on the figures provided above.

WORKERS (INPUTS)	TOTAL PRODUCT	MARGINAL PRODUCT
1		
2		
3		
4		
5		

2. Plot the figures from your table in the graphs below.

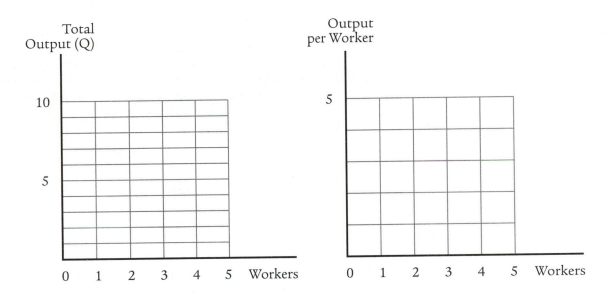

3. Can you identify any relationship between the graphs of marginal product of labor and total product of labor?

4. Look up the definition of diminishing marginal returns in your text. Substitute the links factory terminology for the economics jargon and rewrite the definition. At what point in the typical links factory did diminishing returns set in? _____

5. What do you think would happen to marginal product if we continued to add additional workers? Do you think total product could ever fall? If so, what would have to be true about marginal product to make total product fall?

6. On the graphs for question 2 above, extend the total product and marginal product curves with dotted lines to show what a declining total product curve would look like, and what the marginal product curve would look like if total product did actually decline.

7. Now let us assign numbers to some of your costs. Rent for the desk was $10.00 per period, interest on the loan used to purchase the scissors was $5.00 per period, and labor costs were $10.00 per worker per period. Calculate the missing values in the table below using the data from the typical links factory (not your own) provided above. Treat labor as your only variable input (for simplicity we are disregarding paper costs).

Output	Total Fixed Cost	Total Variable Cost	Total Cost
0	_____	_____	_____
2	_____	_____	_____
6	_____	_____	_____
8	_____	_____	_____
9	_____	_____	_____

8. Plot the figures from your table on the graph.

    Notice that we could derive the total variable cost graph from the total product graph by flipping the axes (placing labor on the vertical and output on the horizontal axis) and multiplying each quantity of labor by the wage to obtain the total variable cost.

9. How are the TC, TVC, and TFC curves related to each other?

10. Suppose that links sell for $7.00 each. How would you determine the total revenue (TR) gained from selling links?

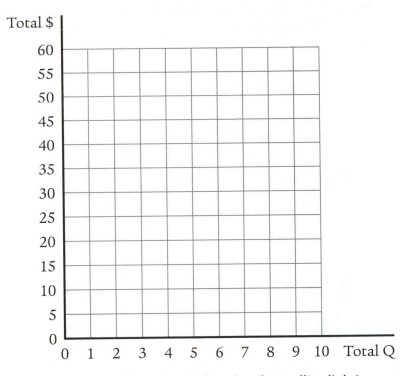

11. How would you determine profit or loss from selling links?

12. Complete the following table. You may obtain the TC figures from the table for question 7 on page 90.

Q	TC	TR	PROFIT/LOSS
0	_____	_____	_____
2	_____	_____	_____
6	_____	_____	_____
8	_____	_____	_____
9	_____	_____	_____

13. If you could produce any of the quantities in this table, what amount would you choose? _____. Why would you not be willing to produce nine and take in more money?

14. Add the total revenue curve to your graph for question 8.

15. What does the vertical distance between TR and TC represent?

16. At what level of output at which TR > TC is the distance between TR and TC the greatest?

17. What is another name for the rate at which TC is changing?

18. What is another name for the rate at which TR is changing?

19. What is the relationship between the rates of change of TR and TC when they are the greatest distance apart?

Afterthoughts

Whew! If you made it this far, you've put in a lot of good work. You have now generated your own economic data and used it to derive many of the important relationships in microeconomics. If you ever have questions or concerns about firm behavior, look back at this experiment and remind yourself where those curves come from and why the slopes and intersections are important. Good work!

Classroom Experiment 4.B

Learning Graphs the Fun Way: Blind Curve

Time Required: *25 minutes*

Materials Required: *one sheet of paper per person and one file folder per two people*

Purpose: *To help students familiarize themselves with complex graphs.*

Level of Difficulty: *low to moderate.*

Textbook Coverage of Underlying Topics:
Arnold Ch. 7, McConnell/Brue Ch. 34, Mankiw Ch. 6, Colander Ch. 11, McEachern Ch. 21, Baumol/Blinder Ch. 8

Introduction

Learning to draw graphs correctly is perhaps the most important skill learned in some economics courses. It can also be the most difficult. This exercise will allow you to practice drawing graphs and will make you think carefully about the relationships between the lines on the graphs. After concentrating on the intersection points and shapes, as you will here, you should have an easier time remembering the accurate relationships and the critical junctures when you go to apply the graphs to answer worthwhile questions.

Scenario

Your instructor will divide the class into pairs of two. You and your partner can then arrange your chairs so that one of you faces the chalkboard and the other faces the back of the room. Your desks should touch each other in the middle. (If you have tables rather than desks with chairs attached, arrange your chairs on either side of the same table.) Place the file folder in between the two of you so that you cannot see the paper on your partner's side of the table/desk. Your instructor will draw a graph on the board, allowing only those facing the board to see it. The objective of the exercise is for the participants who are facing the board to describe the graphs to their partners so that the partners can draw them. Those facing the chalkboard are not to look at the graphs their partners are drawing, and those drawing the graphs are not to look at the chalkboard.

In the event that you are already familiar with the name of the lines on the graph, you are not allowed to convey or inquire about any names. The student who is describing the graph must proceed with phrases like, "The first line starts near the top of the vertical axis. It is a straight line with a slope of about negative one. A second line, with a slope of about positive one, starts just above the origin on the vertical axis and crosses the first line in the middle. A third line starts where the first line started and bisects the distance between the vertical axis and the first line. . . ." Be clear and creative in your explanations. When you think you have completed your artwork, take a look and see how you did. Then switch seats and get ready to do it again with the roles reversed.

Reflections

(Please answer these questions *after* completing the classroom experiment.)

1. How did you do? Was your diagram close to being correct?

2. What is the name of the graph you drew?

3. What is important about the location of the intersection of the lines you drew? (You may look up the graph in your book or notes to learn the answer to this.)

4. What is significant about the slope of the lines you drew? (Ditto)

Afterthoughts

This activity provides a memorable introduction to valuable diagrams. As a positive externality, it is also an excellent exercise in giving instructions. We hope it will help you learn the subtleties of economic models and the pitfalls of common communication.

Problem Set 4.1

The Fixed, Variable, and Total Cost of Production

The table below provides production cost data for a firm.

OUTPUT	VARIABLE COST	FIXED COST	TOTAL COST
0	____	____	100
1	100	____	____
2	175	____	____
3	225	____	____
4	250	____	____
5	260	____	____
6	275	____	____
7	325	____	____
8	400	____	____
9	500	____	____
10	700	____	____

1. Fill in the blanks in Table 4.1

2. Graph variable cost, fixed cost, and total cost on the graph below.

3. What is the relationship (if any) between VC and TC? Why?

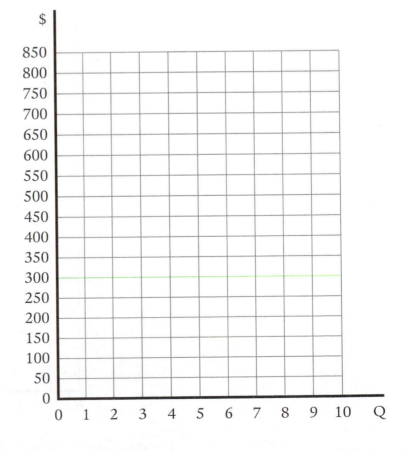

Problem Set 4.2

The Average and Marginal Cost of Production

Use the information in the table in Problem Set 4.1 to answer the following questions.

OUTPUT	AVC	AFC	ATC	MC
1	_____	_____	_____	_____
2	_____	_____	_____	_____
3	_____	_____	_____	_____
4	_____	_____	_____	_____
5	_____	_____	_____	_____
6	_____	_____	_____	_____
7	_____	_____	_____	_____
8	_____	_____	_____	_____
9	_____	_____	_____	_____
10	_____	_____	_____	_____

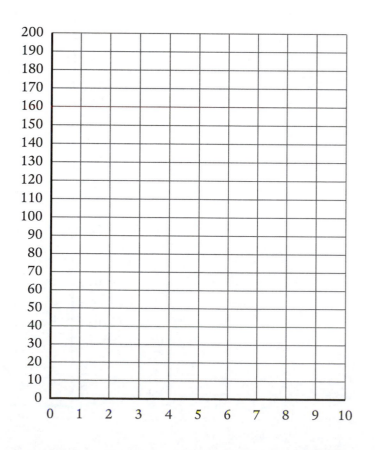

1. Fill in the table.

2. Graph the data from the table on the graph.

3. Why does AFC have the shape that it has?

4. What is the graphical relationship between MC and AVC, if any?

5. What is the graphical relationship between MC and ATC, if any?

6. What is the graphical relationship between MC and AFC, if any?

Problem Set 4.3

Daphne's Apparel Shop 1

Daphne's apparel shop makes women's accessories in a perfectly competitive market. Complete the revenue schedule below.

P	Q	TR ($P \cdot Q$)	AR (TR/Q)	MR ($\Delta TR/\Delta Q$)
$7	0	_____		
$7	1	_____	_____	_____
$7	2	_____	_____	_____
$7	3	_____	_____	_____
$7	4	_____	_____	_____
$7	5	_____	_____	_____
$7	6	_____	_____	_____
$7	7	_____	_____	_____
$7	8	_____	_____	_____
$7	9	_____	_____	_____

1. Graph the total revenue on the graph below.

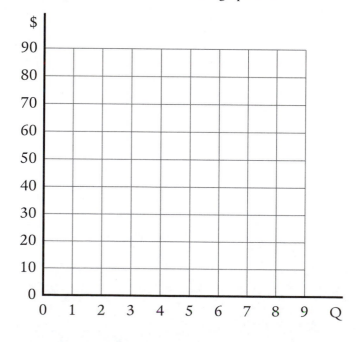

2. Graph the AR, MR, D, and P on the graph below.

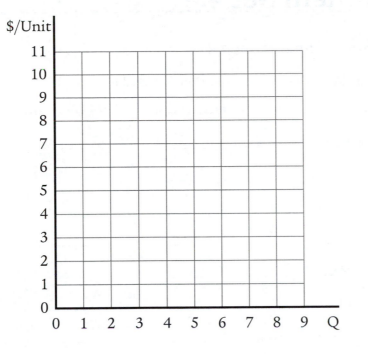

Problem Set 4.4

Daphne's Apparel Shop 2

Classify the following as Fixed Costs or Variable Costs:

Costs	Fixed Costs	Variable Costs
1. Rent	_____	_____
2. Thread	_____	_____
3. Buttons	_____	_____
4. Wages	_____	_____
5. Electricity	_____	_____
6. Cloth	_____	_____
7. Equipment Rent	_____	_____
8. Shipping Costs	_____	_____
9. Insurance	_____	_____
10. Property Taxes	_____	_____

Calculate the following costs for Daphne's apparel shop.

Production	FC	VC	TC
0	_____	_____	5
1	_____	6	_____
2	_____	9	_____
3	_____	13	_____
4	_____	18	_____
5	_____	25	_____
6	_____	34	_____
7	_____	49	_____
8	_____	68	_____

Graph the VC, FC and TC on the graph below.

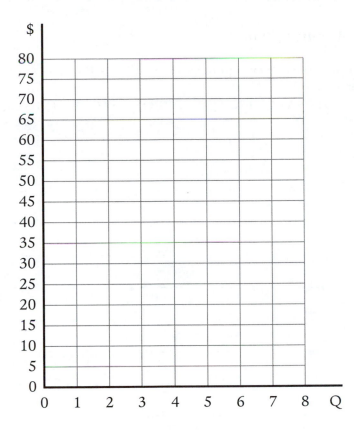

Problem Set 4.5

Daphne's Apparel Shop 3

Complete the following table from the information in Daphne's Apparel Shop parts 1 and 2.

Q	FC	VC	(FC + VC) TC	(FC/Q) AFC	(VC/Q) AVC	(TC/Q) ATC	(ΔTC/ΔQ) MC
0	_____	_____	_____				
1	_____	_____	_____	_____	_____	_____	_____
2	_____	_____	_____	_____	_____	_____	_____
3	_____	_____	_____	_____	_____	_____	_____
4	_____	_____	_____	_____	_____	_____	_____
5	_____	_____	_____	_____	_____	_____	_____
6	_____	_____	_____	_____	_____	_____	_____
7	_____	_____	_____	_____	_____	_____	_____
8	_____	_____	_____	_____	_____	_____	_____

1. Graph the ATC, AVC, AFC, and MC on the graph.

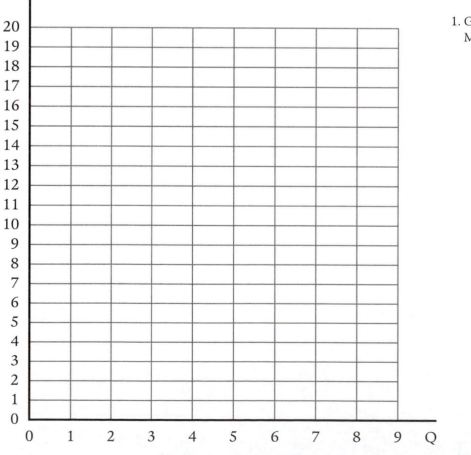

Problem Set 4.6

Daphne's Apparel Shop 4

Complete the following table from the information in Daphne's Apparel Shop parts 1 and 2 with double the fixed costs.

Q	FC	VC	(FC + VC) TC	(FC/Q) AFC	(VC/Q) AVC	(TC/Q) ATC	(ΔTC/ΔQ) MC
0	___	___	___				
1	___	___	___	___	___	___	___
2	___	___	___	___	___	___	___
3	___	___	___	___	___	___	___
4	___	___	___	___	___	___	___
5	___	___	___	___	___	___	___
6	___	___	___	___	___	___	___
7	___	___	___	___	___	___	___
8	___	___	___	___	___	___	___

1. Graph AFC, ATC, AVC, and MC if **Fixed Costs doubled**.

2. Compare this graph with your original Daphne (Part 3).

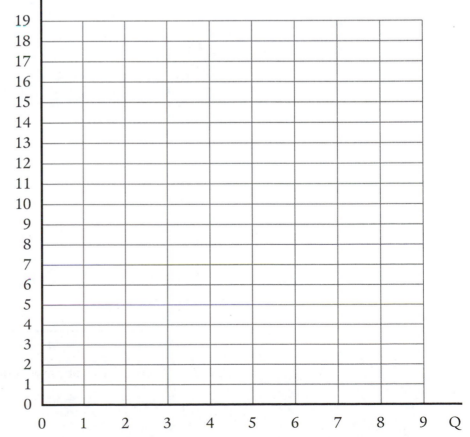

Problem Set 4.7

Daphne's Apparel Shop 5

Complete the following table from the information in Daphne's Apparel Shop parts 1 and 2 with one-half of the original level of variable costs.

Q	FC	VC	(FC + VC) TC	(FC/Q) AFC	(VC/Q) AVC	(TC/Q) ATC	(ΔTC/ΔQ) MC
0	_____	_____	_____				
1	_____	_____	_____	_____	_____	_____	_____
2	_____	_____	_____	_____	_____	_____	_____
3	_____	_____	_____	_____	_____	_____	_____
4	_____	_____	_____	_____	_____	_____	_____
5	_____	_____	_____	_____	_____	_____	_____
6	_____	_____	_____	_____	_____	_____	_____
7	_____	_____	_____	_____	_____	_____	_____
8	_____	_____	_____	_____	_____	_____	_____

1. Graph the AFC, ATC, AVC, and MC when **VC is cut in half.**

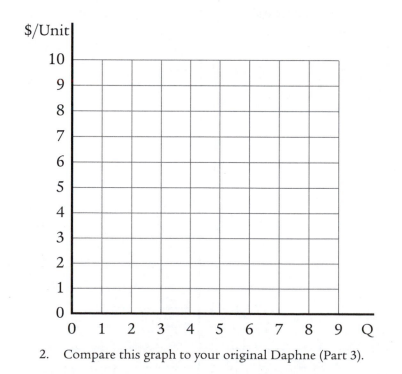

2. Compare this graph to your original Daphne (Part 3).

Problem Set 4.8

Daphne's Apparel Shop 6

Complete the table below using Daphne's Apparel Shop parts 4 and 5, in which fixed costs were doubled and variable costs were cut in half.

Q	FC	VC	TC	ATC	AVC	MC	P	TR	ATR	MR	PROFIT
0											
1											
2											
3											
4											
5											
6											
7											
8											

1. Graph ATC, AVC, MC, ATR, MR, P, and D using the data from the table above.

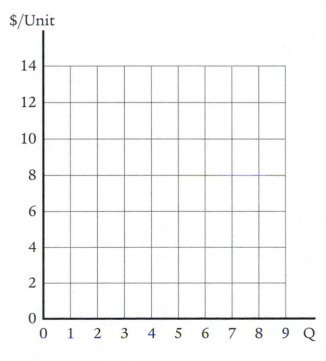

Problem Set 4.9

Cost Curves—The Un-University

Consider the following hypothetical situation. You are in the business of running a fake university. It is a true party school where there are no classes, no exams, no assignments, just dorms and classroom buildings. Students who can't make it anywhere else come to your university to perk up and get a chance at a feeling of being successful again. People over 30 believe you run a legitimate school. Tuition to your school is $30 per month. However, your costs are high. You must pay $50 per month in illegal bribes to the head of the State Board of Certification to maintain your accreditation. Without the bribes, you could not operate at all. You must pay your professors according to the number of "Un-students" they have enrolled. Any student who enrolls in classes but does not attend is an "Un-student." The following table lists the total payment to professors depending on enrollment.

TEACHERS' MONTHLY FEE	NUMBER OF "UN-STUDENTS" ENROLLED
$50	1
$60	2
$70	3
$80	4
$85	5
$87	6
$90	7
$95	8
$100	9
$105	10
$110	11
$115	12

1. Graph TC, FC, VC, and TR on the graph on page 107.

2. How many "Un-students" must you have to break even (rounded down to the nearest whole "Un-student")?

3. What is the smallest number of "Un-students" you would accept and still remain open in the short run (for any one year), rounded down to the nearest whole "Un-student"?

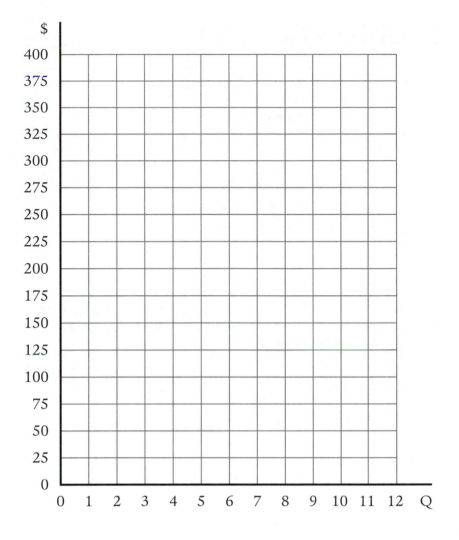

4. What would your answer to question 3 be if the bribe to the Certification Board were to change to $100 per month?

Problem Set 4.10

Perfect Competition Consultants

	PRICE	Q	TR	TC	PROFITS/ LOSSES	TVC	ATC	AVC	MC
1.	4	___	___	___	___	300	3.5	3	5
2.	___	20	200	___	−300	___	___	15	10
3.	___	___	___	5100	−100	3000	___	30	90
4.	25	100	___	___	0	2000	___	20	___

The four perfect competitors shown above have hired you to advise them. The only concern they have is to maximize profits. Based on your analysis of the data for each of their situations, what would you advise each of these firms to do and why?

Firm 1.

Firm 2.

Firm 3.

Firm 4.

Problem Set 4.11

Perfectly Competitive Markets and Firms

1. What is the profit/loss situation for the representative firm whose costs and price are depicted on the right side of the figure below?

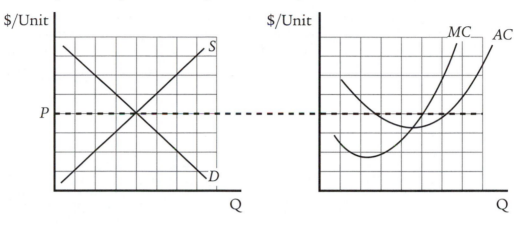

2. How would the market graph on the left side of the figure change in the long run?

3. How would the changes in the market affect individual firms in that market?

4. What is the profit/loss situation for the representative firm whose costs and price are depicted on the right side of the figure below?

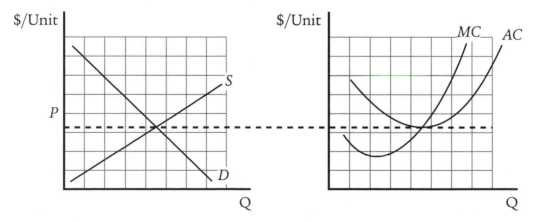

5. Demonstrate how the graphs would change in the short-run if the product being produced in the second figures were to become less popular with consumers.

6. How would the market graph on the left side of the second set of figures change in the long run as the result of the product's decrease in popularity?

Problem Set 4.12

Perfect Competition: Reading the Graphs

Refer to the figure below to answer the following questions.

1. What is the price facing this perfect competitor?

2. What is the average revenue received by this firm?

3. Describe the demand curve facing this firm.

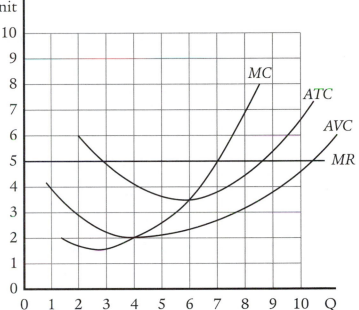

4. What quantity can this perfect competitor sell at the price you indicated in question 1?

5. At what level of output does ATC reach its minimum level?

6. At what level of output does AVC reach its minimum level?

7. At what level of output would this firm chose to operate? Why?

8. At the level of output you indicated in question 7, calculate each of the following.

   a. Total cost

   b. Total revenue

   c. Profit or loss

9. What would happen in the long-run in a market in which all firms found themselves facing a $5 price?

10. If the price facing this firm fell to $3, what would be the values of each of the following at the quantity that the firm would produce?

    a. Total cost

    b. Total revenue

    c. Profit or loss

11. What would happen in the long run in a market in which all firms found themselves facing a $3 price?

12. What is the long-run equilibrium price that would prevail if all firms faced similar cost conditions?

Imperfect Competition 5

Classroom Experiment 5.A

Game Theory and the Prisoners' Oligopoly

> **Time Required:** *20–30 minutes*
>
> **Materials Required:** *scrap paper on which to report the chosen strategy*
>
> **Purpose:** *To provide experience with decision making in the presence of a dominant strategy.*
>
> **Level of Difficulty:** *low to moderate. Players make decisions with interdependent outcomes.*
>
> **Textbook Coverage of Underlying Topics:** *Arnold Ch. 24, McConnell/Brue Ch. 25, Mankiw Ch. 16, Colander Ch. 13, McEachern Ch. 10, Baumol/Blinder Ch. 11*

Introduction

Firm behavior under the conditions of perfect competition and monopoly is predictable. In an oligopolistic market structure—one with a small number of firms that can influence the product price—behavior is harder to pin down. This uncertainty is due to the interdependency of decision making within oligopolies. The best pricing, production, and quality decisions for each firm depend on what other firms are doing. The experiment below will highlight this interdependency and allow you to experience the dilemmas faced by the managers of oligopolistic firms.

Scenario

In this experiment, you will wear two different hats. You can ease into interdependence in the first part of the experiment by playing yourself—a student trying to maximize her or his grade. You and your adversaries will independently select a grade of A, B, or C. These grade selections will be placed into a hat, and then random selections will pair you with a specific adversary to determine your final grade on the experiment. (There might also be a second round in which you will know who your adversary is before deciding on your strategy.) The payoff matrix below indicates what your final grade will be, depending on which grade you and your adversary select. Note that if your adversary picks C, your final grade will be the grade you chose. If your adversary picks B, your final grade will be one grade below the grade you chose. And if your adversary picks A, your final grade will be an F. Even though you will not know your adversary's strategy until after you have picked a grade, you might want to consider your best strategy given each possible choice made by your adversary. That is, if she picks C, what is your best choice, and so on.

| | | YOUR SELECTION | | |
		A	B	C
YOUR ADVERSARY'S SELECTION	A	You receive: F Adversary: F	You receive: F Adversary: B	You receive: F Adversary: A
	B	You receive: B Adversary: F	You receive: C Adversary: C	You receive: D Adversary: B
	C	You receive: A Adversary: F	You receive: B Adversary: D	You receive: C Adversary: C

After you have made your selection, record it on a sheet of paper along with your name and hand it in. Your instructor will make *random pairings* and report your grades to you.

For the second part of this experiment, you will be acting as an oligopolist in an industry with two firms. You have the task of deciding whether to charge high or low prices. Each of the two firms must decide which prices to publish in the newspaper a few days before the paper comes out. Thus, they must make the decision without knowing what prices the other side will advertise. Even if they call each other and agree on one price, the incentives to lie make such agreements untrustworthy. If one of you charges high prices and the other charges low prices, the one with the low prices will steal away most of the competition and make $120 in profits today, while the one with the high prices earns only $50 in profits. If both charge high prices, the combined profits are larger, but no firm earns as much as if it were offering relatively attractive prices. With both charging low prices, profits are smaller than if both charged high prices but better than those earned by a firm charging higher prices than its competitor. The payoff matrix below summarizes the interdependent outcomes.

| | | YOUR PRICE | |
		HIGH	LOW
COMPETITOR'S PRICE	HIGH	Your profit: $100 Competitor's: $100	Your profit: $120 Competitor's: $50
	LOW	Your profit: $50 Competitor's: $120	Your profit: $80 Competitor's: $80

After you have made your selection, record it on the recording sheet along with your name and hand it in. Your instructor will make random pairings and report your profits to you.

Reflections

(Please answer these questions *after* completing the classroom experiment.)

1. In the results for your class, how common were failing grades and low prices?

2. How would you explain the outcomes discussed in question 1? That is, why didn't people adopt the strategies that would lead to higher grades and profits for everyone?

3. A dominant strategy is one that is best regardless of the other side's strategy. What is the dominant strategy in the grade experiment? _____ What is the dominant strategy in the pricing experiment? _____

4. Who gains and who loses from the difficulty of coordinating strategies among oligopolists?

5. Can you think of other situations in which undesirable dominant strategies result in sub-optimal outcomes?

Afterthoughts

Your experience in these experiments provides insight into the strategizing of oligopolists and helps to explain why we sometimes see low prices even when firms would earn more profits with high prices. Dominant strategy equilibria, such as those, help to explain many other suboptimal phenomena, such as the wearing of expensive and uncomfortable clothes to interviews and studying hard in a class that is graded on a curve. Can you draw a payoff matrix for one of these situations that indicates why?

If you enjoyed this exercise, you might consider similar prisoners' dilemma activities available on the Web (e.g., http://serendip.bryn-mawr.edu/playground/pd.html) and in Margaret A. Ray's article, "Oligopoly and Interdependence in the Classroom," 2(2) *Classroom Expernomics*, Fall 1993, (http://www.marietta.edu/~delemeeg/exper-nom/f93.html).

Classroom Experiment 5.B

A Cartel Growing Bananas

Time Required: *5–10 minutes*	**Textbook Coverage of Underlying Topics:** *Arnold Ch. 24,*
Materials Required: *scrap paper to use as production-report sheets*	*McConnell/Brue Ch. 25, Mankiw Ch. 16, Colander Ch. 13, McEachern Ch. 10,*
Purpose: *To demonstrate the temptation to cheat within a cartel.*	*Baumol/Blinder Ch. 11*
Level of Difficulty: *low to moderate.*	

Introduction

Oligopoly firms sometimes face the temptation of colluding together, legally or illegally, and act like a monopoly. If successful, this would allow them to earn the same level of profits that a monopoly would, and these profits could be divided among the firms in a mutually beneficial manner. A group of firms working together in this way is called a cartel. OPEC, the Organization of Petroleum Exporting Countries, exemplifies both the intent and the pitfalls of cartels. Before you read more about this market structure, it will be informative to wear a cartel member's shoes for a while.

Scenario

You will soon meet in Geneva with fellow members of the Bananas Independently Grown (BIG) cartel. The president of your cartel, your instructor, has a proposal for you to consider that s/he states will allow your cartel to gain more profits to be divided among the members. After listening to the proposal, you will be asked to report your production level for the subsequent period as a percentage of your usual production level. For example, if you will produce half of your usual amount, write down 50 person. If you will produce the same amount as before, write down 100 person, and so on. In addition to the options presented by your cartel president, you should also be aware of incentives to cheat. That is, at least in the short run, you can produce additional bananas beyond the proposed limit and ship them off in the dark of night at a price close to the cartel price. This will earn you some extra cash, but if many of the cartel members do this, too many bananas will be supplied and the intended monopoly-level price and the corresponding profits will fall for everyone. Listen to your president's ideas and then write down the actual percentage of your usual banana crop that you will produce next period. Your production report will be completely anonymous.

Reflections

(Please answer these questions *after* completing the classroom experiment.)

1. Describe the outcome of your cartel experiment.

2. What was your production level, and what motivated you to produce that amount?

3. Who benefits and who is harmed by greed among members of a cartel?

4. Who benefits and who is harmed by profit maximization by a monopoly?

5. Do you have any ideas for how to handle the problem of greed when it is destructive?

Afterthoughts

Indeed, cartels like OPEC are seldom able to restrict the quantity produced to the mutually beneficial levels. They typically end up producing too much (from the sellers' standpoint) and earning less than planned. The difficulty of monitoring the output of member nations can cause insurmountable temptation, as greed is all too often the overarching motivator. Fortunately for consumers, cartel failure results in lower prices and higher quantities than if the ventures were to succeed.

Classroom Experiment 5.C

A Monopoly Making Dough

Time Required: *15–20 minutes (less if the table is filled in before class)*	Level of Difficulty: *moderate*
Materials: *none*	**Textbook Coverage of Underlying Concepts:** *Arnold Ch. 23, McConnell/Brue Ch. 24, Mankiw Ch. 15, Colander Ch. 12, McEachern Ch. 9, Baumol/Blinder Ch. 10*
Purpose: *To provide insight into the forces of market structure, including the influence of monopoly on price and quantity.*	

Introduction

Perhaps you've been in an airport where a single pizza purveyor represents the only choice for those in the mood for food. And then there are the business districts brimming with pizza shops where you can buy a whole pie for about the price of a piece in the airport. What's the deal with that? Is it natural? Is it good economics? Let's find out!

Scenario

Phase I—The Monopoly. You make pizza like no other. Your product is inches thick, dripping with cheese, and bursting with flavor from a secret ingredient Colonel Sanders would have given his right wing for. Your exclusive human capital—talents and secrets—give you a monopoly on the gourmet pizza business in your area, and you face the entire market demand for gourmet pizza as illustrated in the graph below. Be sure to read the graph correctly. It indicates that you can sell one pizza for $10, or two for $9 each, or three for $8 each, and so on.

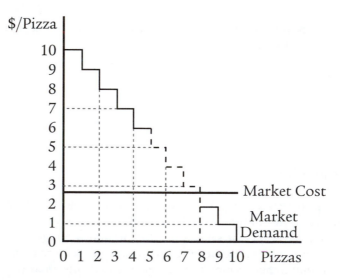

Each pizza costs $2.50 to make. What price and corresponding quantity should you choose to maximize profits? In order to find out, fill in the following table and add the marginal revenue and marginal cost curves to the diagram above:

PIZZAS	TOTAL REVENUE	MARGINAL REVENUE	TOTAL COST	MARGINAL COST	PROFIT
1					
2					
3					
4					
5					
6					
7					
8					
9					
10					

Remember:

> **Total revenue** is price times quantity.
>
> **Marginal revenue** is the total revenue from a given quantity minus the total revenue when selling one pizza fewer.
>
> **Total cost** is the sum of all costs associated with making a given quantity.
>
> **Marginal cost** is the total cost of a given quantity minus the total cost when making one pizza fewer.

What is your optimal price? _____ How many will you sell at that price? _____

Phase II—Competitors Enter. Few secrets allude the information age, and alas, a disgruntled worker at your pizzeria has shared your baking secrets on the Internet. Everyone in the class is now a potential entrant into the gourmet pizza market. Everyone's marginal cost is $2.50. As always, this includes the opportunity cost of your time. Thus, if you can get at least $2.50 per pizza, there's nothing else you could do with your time to earn more money.

Your instructor represents the consumers in the market. All existing pizza makers are assumed to make pizza of identical quality, and the consumers will purchase from whoever has the lowest price. As your instructor inquires about available prices, you have the option to enter the pizza market or not depending on the going price. When more than one pizzeria is operating, the consumer demand is divided evenly among the existing pizzerias.

Reflections

1. You have studied firm behavior in your textbook. When you chose your profit-maximizing price and quantity as a monopolist, did your behavior correspond with the rules for profit maximization explained in your textbook? Explain.

2. Describe the result of entry into the gourmet pizza market—what changed?

3. Do your findings agree with economic theory in terms of the price in a competitive market and the influence of competition on quantity?

4. Who benefits and who loses due to the introduction of competition?

5. Some say the best pizza comes from Chicago or New York, and not from the monopolist at the airport. Could market structure have something to do with this as well? Explain.

6. As an entrepreneur working on innovative recipes (or pharmaceuticals or whatever), how are one's incentives improved by the ability to operate a monopoly?

7. What solutions or compromises would you suggest to resolve this dilemma between the costs and benefits of market power?

Afterthoughts

This experiment highlights the influence of market power. Your findings help to explain both the corporate battles for patents, mergers, and acquisitions, and the enactment of antitrust legislation to prevent excessive market power. For example, the McDonald's Corporation acquired fast-food competitor Domino's Pizza, Inc., while the U.S. took up a case against the powerful Microsoft Corporation. Antitrust policy and enforcement decisions are common and important, which is why it's wise for you to have insight into the importance and dynamics of market power.

Problem Set 5.1

Daphne's Apparel Shop as a Monopoly

Complete the table below.

Q	FC	VC	TC	ATC	AVC	MC	P	TR	ATR	MR	Profit
0	5	___	___				13	___			___
1	___	6	___	___	___	___	12	___	___	___	___
2	___	9	___	___	___	___	11	___	___	___	___
3	___	13	___	___	___	___	10	___	___	___	___
4	___	18	___	___	___	___	9	___	___	___	___
5	___	25	___	___	___	___	8	___	___	___	___
6	___	34	___	___	___	___	7	___	___	___	___
7	___	49	___	___	___	___	6	___	___	___	___
8	___	68	___	___	___	___	5	___	___	___	___

1. Graph the ATC, AVC, MC, ATR, MR, P, and D.

2. Determine the profit-maximizing output and price this monopolist will charge.

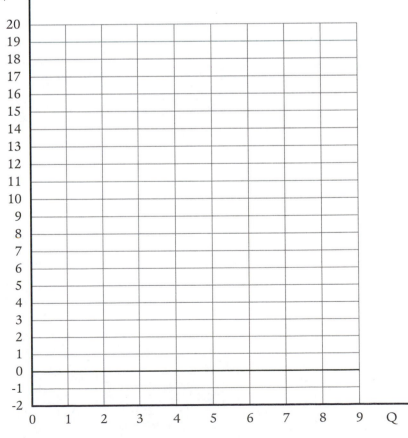

Problem Set 5.2

Monopoly Consultant

	P	MR	Q	TR	TC	P/L	TVC	ATC	AVC	MC
1.	10	5	___	100	___	+50	30	___	___	7
2.	50	<___	___	2500	2600	___	___	52	32	50
3.	___	5	___	___	8000	+2000	5000	8	5 (min)	___
4.	90	70	___	2250	___	+750	___	60	50	50

The four monopolists shown above have hired you to advise them. The only concern they have is to maximize profits. Based on your analysis of the data what would you advise each of these firms to do and why?

Firm 1.

Firm 2.

Firm 3.

Firm 4.

Problem Set 5.3

Monopoly

Please answer the following questions on the basis of the graph provided.

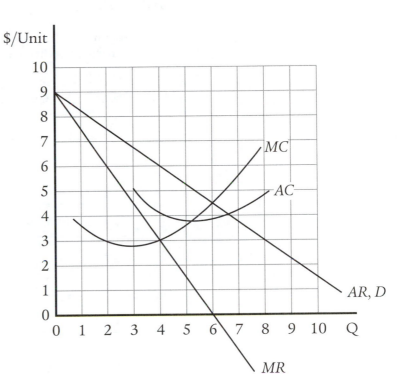

1. What price could this monopolist charge for the good being sold?

2. What quantity of the good would this profit-maximizing monopolist sell? Why?

3. What price would this profit-maximizing monopolist charge for the good? Why?

4. Indicate the values for the following items at the quantity you identified in Question 2:

   a. Marginal revenue

   b. Marginal cost

   c. Average revenue

   d. Price

   e. Average cost

   f. Total revenue

   g. Total cost

   h. Total

   i. Profit per unit

5. Is there any price and quantity combination at which this monopolist would break-even?

Problem Set 5.4

Total Revenue, Marginal Revenue, and Average Revenue

Assume that the following figures are for a monopolist who has just introduced a patented product. Market research shows the following:

PRICE	QUANTITY	TOTAL REVENUE	MARGINAL REVENUE	AVERAGE REVENUE
$11	0			
$10	1			
$9	2			
$8	3			
$7	4			
$6	5			
$5	6			
$4	7			
$3	8			
$2	9			
$1	10			

1.   Calculate and fill in the blanks for total revenue.

2.   Calculate and fill in the blanks for marginal revenue.

3.   Calculate and fill in the blanks for average revenue.

4.   Graph marginal revenue.

5.   Graph average revenue.

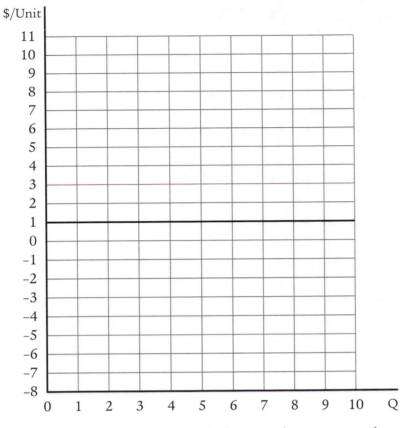

6. How is it possible that marginal revenue becomes zero when the price is positive?

7. What is the meaning of a negative marginal revenue number? How is it possible that marginal revenue turns negative? What does a negative marginal revenue imply about the price elasticity of demand?

8. Why is marginal revenue below average revenue for a monopolist?

Problem Set 5.5

Marginal Revenue and Elasticity

To answer the following questions use the figures for total revenue and marginal revenue from Problem Set 5.4, "Total Revenue, Marginal Revenue, and Average Revenue."

1. Please fill in the blanks with the appropriate total revenue and price elasticity figures.

   a. At a price of $1, total revenue is

       At a price of $2, total revenue is

       Therefore in this price range the demand curve is

   b. At a price of $2, total revenue is

       At a price of $3, total revenue is

       Therefore in this price range the demand curve is

   c. At a price of $3, total revenue is

       At a price of $4, total revenue is

       Therefore in this price range the demand curve is

   d. At a price of $4, total revenue is

       At a price of $5, total revenue is

       Therefore in this price range the demand curve is

   e. At a price of $5, total revenue is

       At a price of $6, total revenue is

       Therefore in this price range the demand curve is

   f. At a price of $7, total revenue is

       At a price of $8, total revenue is

       Therefore in this price range the demand curve is

   g. At a price of $8, total revenue is

       At a price of $9, total revenue is

       Therefore in this price range the demand curve is

   h. At a price of $9, total revenue is

       At a price of $10, total revenue is

       Therefore, in this price range, the demand curve is

2. List all price ranges in which demand is elastic.

3. List all price ranges in which demand is inelastic.

4. Are there any price ranges in which demand is neither elastic nor inelastic? If so, what label applies to the elasticity of demand in those price ranges?

5. What is true about marginal revenue when demand is elastic?

6. What is true about marginal revenue when demand is inelastic?

7. What is true about marginal revenue when demand is unit elastic?

8. Would a monopolist ever willingly operate on the inelastic portion of his or her demand curve? Why or why not?

9. Would a monopolist ever willingly operate on the elastic portion of his or her demand curve? Could the same conclusion be drawn about the elastic portion of the demand curve as was drawn in the previous question about the inelastic portion? Why or why not?

Problem Set 5.6

Game Theory

The following chart lists expected profits for your firm and your rival depending on each side's advertising strategy. In each square, the profit identified in the upper-right goes to you, and the profit identified in the lower left goes to your rival. For example, if you don't advertise and your rival doesn't advertise, your sales will be less than if you did advertise, but so will your advertising costs. The result will be that each of you will earn a $75 profit. If you advertise and your rival does not, you will gain a lot of customers and earn a $100 profit, while your rival will only earn $10, and so on as you can see from the chart.

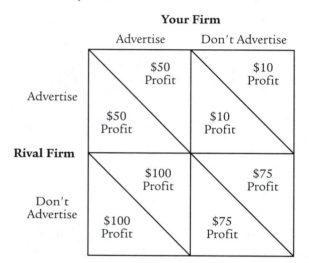

What advertising strategy will you and your rival choose? Why?

Problem Set 5.7

Monopolistic Competition

1. If the curves in Figure 1 are for a monopolistic competitor, is this a long-run or a short-run outcome? What is the profit/loss situation for this firm?

2. Given what you have learned from your textbook about monopolistically competitive markets, what will happen next if the short-run situation is as shown in Figure 1?

3. Suppose that the situation changes to that described in Figure 2. Interpret the new profit/loss situation for this monopolistic competitor.

4. Given what you have learned from your textbook about monopolistically competitive markets, what will happen next if the short-run situation is as shown in Figure 2?

5. Suppose that the situation changes to that described in Figure 3. Interpret the new profit/loss situation for this monopolistic competitor. Is this necessarily a short-run situation?

6. What will happen in a monopolistically competitive market in which individual firms are in the situation illustrated in Figure 3?

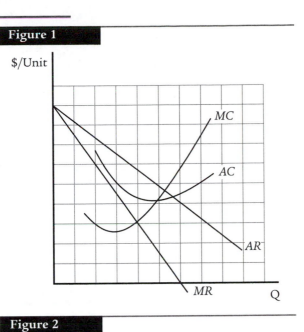

Figure 1

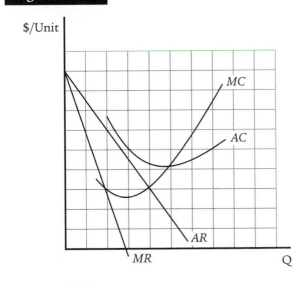

Figure 2

Figure 3

7.   What can you conclude about the behavior of individual firms in a monopolistically competitive market in the short run and in the long run?

Problem Set 5.8

Changing Variable Cost and Fixed Cost

Throughout this problem set, assume that the product can only be sold in whole units.

CHANGING VARIABLE COST AND FIXED COST

P	Q	TR	MR	AR	FC_1	FC_2	VC_1	VC_2	TC_1	TC_2	TC_3	TC_4	MC_1	MC_2	MC_3	MC_4
12	0				5	10	0	0								
11	1						5	10								
10	2						9	18								
9	3						12	24								
8	4						14	27								
7	5						15	31								
6	6						17	36								
5	7						21	44								
4	8						27	53								
3	9						35	63								
2	10						45	83								
1	11						57	113								

1. Fill in the blanks in the table.

2. Using fixed cost 1 and variable cost 1, what is the profit-maximizing output and price?

3. Using fixed cost 2 and variable cost 1, what is the profit-maximizing output and price?

4. Using fixed cost 1 and variable cost 2, what is the profit-maximizing output and price?

5. Using fixed cost 2 and variable cost 2, what is the profit-maximizing output and price?

6. What can you conclude about the effect that a change in fixed cost has on the profit-maximizing output and price? How does changing fixed cost affect profit?

7. What can you conclude about the effect that changing variable cost has on the profit-maximizing output and price? How does changing variable cost affect profit?

Factor Markets 6

Classroom Experiment 6.A

Deriving the Labor Supply Curve: Put Your Hands Up

Time Required: *10–15 minutes*	**Textbook Coverage of Underlying Topics:**
Materials Required: *none*	Arnold Ch. 26, McConnell/Brue Ch. 28, Mankiw Ch. 18, Colander Ch. 16, McEachern Ch. 12, Baumol/Blinder Ch. 16
Purpose: *To derive a labor supply curve and provide insight into the market for labor.*	
Level of Difficulty: *low to moderate*	

Introduction

The demand curve for labor is derived by simply multiplying the marginal product of labor (as you may have derived for yourself in the Econville Link Factory experiment, discussed in Classroom Experiment 4.A) by the marginal revenue (which is equivalent to the price for competitive firms) earned from sales of the good being produced. In this experiment, we will derive a labor supply curve in a straightforward manner. As potential or actual labor market participants ourselves, it is not difficult for us to think about the wage that would get us to work at all or to work more than we do. Given the available wages and employment opportunities, we regularly face decisions about how much to work. This experiment will make use of what may be well-thought-out thresholds for your willingness to work.

Scenarios

In some employment settings, such as those involving migrant farm workers, foremen come before groups of potential workers and call out increasing wage offers until enough laborers step forward to meet the employer's needs. This experiment will be similar, except that the number of workers willing to provide a day's work will be recorded for each wage, with no goals in terms of the total number of workers willing to work. For the purposes of the experiment, imagine that you are considering employment at the local pizzeria.

Scenario 1. Suppose that besides the pizza shop, the other employment opportunities are no different than the opportunities you presently face in reality. Think for a moment, and then write down the lowest amount of money that the pizza shop could pay you to make pizzas for them this Saturday from 8 A.M. to 5 P.M. with a one-hour lunch. This is a daily wage, not an hourly wage. (Assume that this lowest amount will not affect the actual amount that you receive, so there is no benefit in overstating the minimum you would accept.)

Scenario 2. Now imagine that in addition to the other things you could be doing on Saturday, your favorite television program will air its season finale in mid-afternoon. What is the lowest amount the pizza shop could pay you to work from 8 A.M. to 5 P.M. on Saturday?

Scenario 3. As a last scenario, suppose that your favorite TV program will NOT be on this Saturday but that you just wrecked your car, and within 30 days you must pay $1000 towards higher insurance rates, damage deductibles, and moving violation fines. What is the lowest payment that would motivate you to want to work this Saturday from 8 A.M. to 5 P.M.?

The numbers you have written down are called *reservation wages*, meaning that you would work for those amounts or anything more, but you would not work for anything less than those amounts. Now, as your instructor/foreman calls out various daily wages for working in the pizza shop, raise your hand (the one you don't write with) the first time the daily wage *equals or exceeds* your reservation wage. For example, if your reservation wage is $13, raise your hand when your foreman says $15. With your other hand, record the total number of people willing to work at each wage. This is the sum of those willing to work at the previous wage and the new workers added at the current wage.

WAGE	TOTAL WORKERS SCENARIO 1	TOTAL WORKERS SCENARIO 2	TOTAL WORKERS SCENARIO 3
0	————	————	————
5	————	————	————
10	————	————	————
15	————	————	————
20	————	————	————
25	————	————	————
30	————	————	————
35	————	————	————
40	————	————	————

WAGE	TOTAL WORKERS SCENARIO 1	TOTAL WORKERS SCENARIO 2	TOTAL WORKERS SCENARIO 3
45	_____	_____	_____
50	_____	_____	_____
55	_____	_____	_____
60	_____	_____	_____
65	_____	_____	_____
70	_____	_____	_____
75	_____	_____	_____
80	_____	_____	_____
85	_____	_____	_____
90	_____	_____	_____
95	_____	_____	_____
100	_____	_____	_____

Reflections

(Please answer these questions *after* completing the classroom experiment.)

1. On the diagram below, graph the labor market supply curves for each of the scenarios.

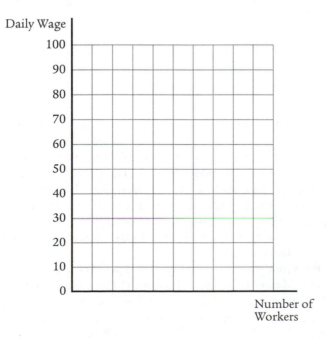

2. Why do you suppose some people had lower reservation wages than others?

3. Describe what happened to your reservation wage in Scenario 2 relative to Scenario 1 and why. Did your classmates behave similarly?

4. Describe what happened to your reservation wage in Scenario 3 relative to Scenario 1 and why. Did your classmates behave similarly?

5. Relative to Scenario 1, what happened to the number of workers supplied at most wage levels in Scenario 2? Can you think of another influence that might have a similar effect on the market labor supply curve?

6. Relative to Scenario 1, what happened to the number of workers supplied at most wage levels in Scenario 3? Can you think of another influence that might have a similar effect on the market labor supply curve?

Afterthoughts

In the real labor market, the decision of whether or not to work on a given day is complicated by opportunities to work part-time, full-time, and overtime and sometimes (particularly for the self-employed) by decisions on exactly how many hours to work. There may also be flexibility in the number of days worked. Nonetheless, the labor supply curve is constructed just as you have done so—the total amount of labor that workers are willing to supply is graphed at each possible wage. Equilibrium in the labor market is achieved at the intersection of this curve and the labor market demand curve.

For a more in-depth labor market experiment, see Michael J. Haupert's "Labor Market Experiment," *Journal of Economic Education*, Fall 1990, p. 300.

Classroom Experiment 6.B

Learning from Teaching: The Anti-REM Game

Time Required: *30 minutes*	**Textbook Coverage of Underlying Topics:** *Arnold Ch. 28, McConnell/Brue Ch. 6, Mankiw Ch. 24, Colander Ch. 24, McEachern Ch. 14, Baumol/Blinder Ch. 26*
Materials Required: *none*	
Purpose: *To reinforce difficult concepts by having students teach them to each other.*	
Level of Difficulty: *moderate*	

Introduction

This game grew out of the authors' belief that just as there is REM (rapid eye movement) sleep, there is REM (really elsewhere mode) class participation. The authors of this book have spent many thousands of hours in class. Believe us, we can daydream with the best of them. When you're concentrating more on an upcoming vacation, meal, or social interaction than on an important lecture, the Anti-REM game is the antidote.

Scenario

You will be randomly paired with a classmate for this exercise. One member of each pair will go outside the classroom and think deep thoughts or quietly discuss how to save (conquer?) the world for five minutes or so while the other member of each pair learns a new and exciting economics topic. When the ousted half of each pair is invited back into the classroom, it is the task of the learned half to teach their ousted partners the concept they just learned. After five minutes or so of intensive teaching and learning, the ousted crew that was taught by the learned few will be asked to respond to a few questions on the material.

Reflections

(Please answer these questions *after* completing the classroom experiment.)

1. What is the concept you learned, and why is it important?

2. Do incentives matter? In other words, how did your obligation to teach or be tested on the material affect your attention to the material being presented?

3. Assuming that those who became student-teachers learned the economic content of the exercise better than the average student trying to learn from passive reading and lectures, how could you alter your typical study routine to reap the same benefits?

Afterthoughts

With luck you have learned two valuable lessons from this exercise. First, you have obtained a solid understanding of an important economic concept. And second, you have picked up a new tool for your bag of learning tricks. Instructors know well that teaching a concept is a great way to force yourself to learn it. When you know you have to explain something to others, you don't let yourself get away with skimming and partial comprehension. Sometimes even explaining something to yourself, as you can when you take notes in your own words on concepts explained in your textbook, will solidify ideas and allow difficult ideas to fit together in a way that just can't happen while you're daydreaming about fudge brownies, for example.

Problem Set 6.1

Total Product and Marginal Product

Assume that the following table lists the total output of the Julie Anne Factory.

QUANTITY OF LABOR	TOTAL OUTPUT	MARGINAL OUTPUT
0	0	
1	100	_____
2	350	_____
3	550	_____
4	650	_____
5	700	_____
6	700	_____
7	650	_____
8	550	_____

1. Fill in the blanks in the table.

2. On the graph below, plot the total product of labor curve.

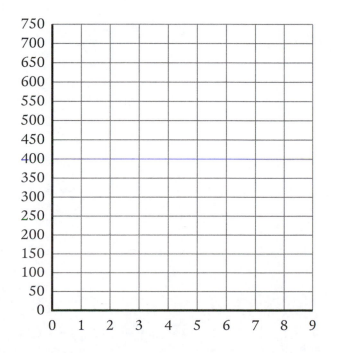

3. On the graph below, plot the marginal physical product of labor curve. See graph

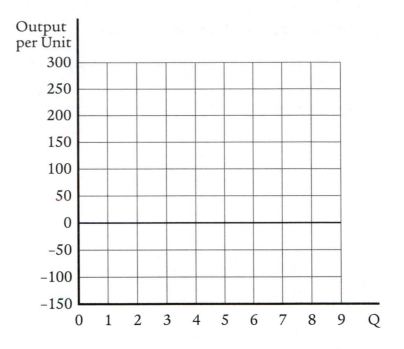

4. At what point do diminishing marginal returns set in?

5. How were you able to determine where diminishing marginal returns set in?

Problem Set 6.2

More on Marginal Product

The following table is for a perfectly competitive firm.

QUANTITY OF LABOR	TOTAL OUTPUT
0	0
1	5
2	15
3	30
4	40
5	45
6	45
7	40

1. Calculate the additional output (marginal physical product) attributable to each worker.

2. At what point (if any) do diminishing returns set in? How were you able to determine that?

3. If this product sells for $5.00 each, calculate the value of the margin-
   al product of labor in the table below.

QUANTITY OF LABOR	VALUE OF THE MARGINAL PRODUCT
0	
1	_____
2	_____
3	_____
4	_____
5	_____
6	_____
7	_____

4. If each worker receives a wage of $40, how many workers will a
   profit-maximizing firm hire? Why?

5. If the product price were to increase to $10 each, how would that
   affect the answer to question 4?

Problem Set 6.3

Derived Demand

Complete the following table for a perfectly competitive firm.

Quantity of Resource	Total Product	Marginal Product	Product Price	Value of Marginal Product
0	0		$5.00	
1	5	_____	_____	_____
2	15	_____	_____	_____
3	30	_____	_____	_____
4	40	_____	_____	_____
5	45	_____	_____	_____
6	45	_____	_____	_____

1. Fill in the blanks in the table.

2. The value of the marginal product of labor *is* the demand for labor. The value of the marginal product of labor is the marginal physical product of labor times the product price. Plot the demand for labor on the graph below.

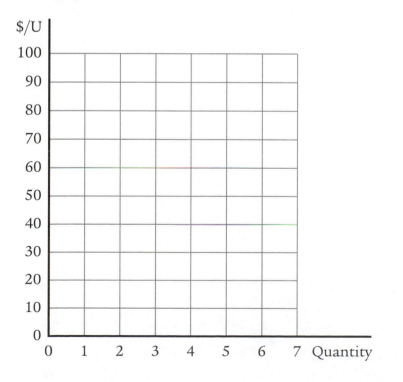

3. Indicate what (if anything) would happen to the demand for labor after each of the following.

    a. An increase in worker productivity

    b. An increase in the popularity of the product

    c. A decrease in worker motivation and interest in the job

    d. The introduction of new technology that makes workers able to produce more in a given amount of time

    e. A decrease in the price of the product

Problem Set 6.4

Changing Marginal Physical Product and Product Price

1. Use economic terminology to explain how a worker training program that increased the productivity of labor would affect the demand for labor?

2. Suppose that starting with the data from Problem Set 6.3, workers become twice as productive after completing a training program. Calculate the new value of their marginal product and regraph the demand for labor that would result.

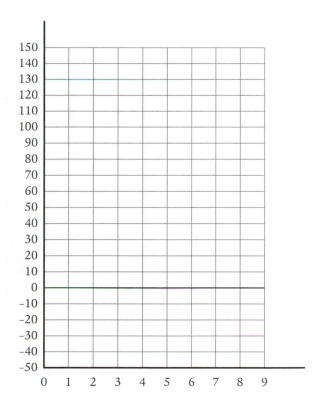

QUANTITY OF RESOURCE	TOTAL PRODUCT OLD	TOTAL PRODUCT NEW	MARGINAL PRODUCT OLD	MARGINAL PRODUCT NEW	PRODUCT PRICE OLD	PRODUCT PRICE NEW	VALUE OF MARGINAL PRODUCT	
0	0	_____						
1	5	_____	5	_____	5	_____	_____	_____
2	15	_____	10	_____	5	_____	_____	_____
3	30	_____	15	_____	5	_____	_____	_____
4	40	_____	10	_____	5	_____	_____	_____
5	45	_____	5	_____	5	_____	_____	_____
6	45	_____	0	_____	5	_____	_____	_____
7	40	_____	–5	_____	5	_____	_____	_____

3. How would an increase in the price of the product being sold affect the demand for labor?

4. Starting with the original marginal physical product numbers from Problem Set 6.3, calculate the effect of an increase in the product price from $5.00 to $7.50 and re-graph the demand for labor that would result.

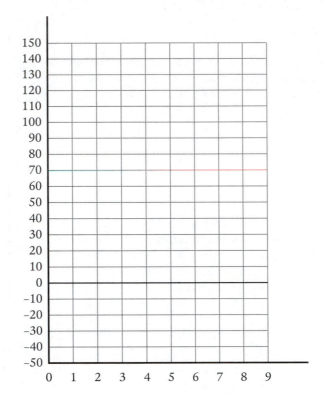

Problem Set 6.5

The Optimum Resource Mix

As a recent graduate of the Graduate School of Business at the University of Northern Freshwater, you have been hired as a consultant. Your first project is to organize production for a manufacturing firm at each of its five plants. Your project goal is to reach targeted amounts of production while achieving minimum resource cost. The figures provided are the amounts of various inputs presently used in the production process at each plant.

The inputs used are priced as follows:

       Land: $5 per hour

       Labor: $10 per hour

       Capital: $25 per hour

	MARGINAL PHYSICAL PRODUCT OF LAND	MARGINAL PHYSICAL PRODUCT OF LABOR	MARGINAL PHYSICAL PRODUCT OF CAPITAL
Facility A	15	50	100
Facility B	40	40	75
Facility C	10	20	125
Facility D	20	40	100
Facility E	40	20	75

1. Which facility or facilities (if any) are presently producing using the least-cost combination of inputs?

2. What specific recommendation would you make for each facility to help them achieve the least-cost combination of resource use?

   a. Recommendation for Facility A

   b. Recommendation for Facility B

c.   Recommendation for Facility C

d.   Recommendation for Facility D

e.   Recommendation for Facility E

Problem Set 6.6

The Unemployment Rate and the Minimum Wage

Use the information in the graph below to answer the following questions. Please refer to the letters provided along the horizontal axis when discussing quantities of labor.

1. What is the quantity of labor employed at the equilibrium wage?

2. If a minimum wage is set at Wage (minimum wage), what would be the quantity of labor demanded?

3. If a minimum wage is set at Wage (minimum wage), what would be the quantity of labor supplied?

4. How many people would become unemployed as a result of the minimum wage?

5. Of those who became unemployed, how many had a job and then lost that job as a result of the minimum wage?

6. Referring to the graph below, if a minimum wage is imposed as shown, how will its effect be different if the demand for labor is represented by Labor Demand A versus Labor Demand B?

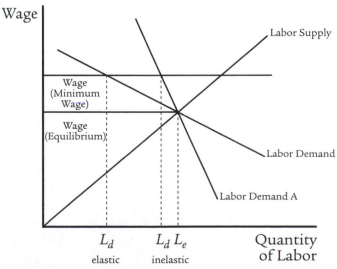

7. Opponents of a minimum wage law would argue that the demand for labor more closely resembles which labor demand curve?

8. Proponents of a minimum wage law would argue that the demand for labor more closely resembles which labor demand curve?

The Public Sector and Market Failure 7

Classroom Experiment 7.A

Free Rider Experiment: Show Me the Money

Time Required: *10 minutes*	**Level of Difficulty:** *low*
Materials Required: *recording sheets (scrap paper)*	**Textbook Coverage of Underlying Topics:** *Arnold Ch. 30, McConnell/Brue Ch. 30, Mankiw Ch. 11, Colander Ch. 18, McEachern Ch. 16, Baumol/Blinder Ch. 12*
Purpose: *To demonstrate the temptation to free ride and the trouble it creates.*	

Introduction

This experiment speaks to the appropriate treatment of public goods. Public goods are those which no one can be excluded from using, and whose values to any particular user are not diminished by the goods' use by other users. National defense and lighthouses are classic examples. Once a lighthouse is erected, no ship can be prevented from benefiting from its guidance, and use of the lighthouse by one ship does not detract from its use by other ships. Most goods, like chocolate bars, are not public goods—you can exclude others from eating your chocolate, and if you eat your chocolate bar, its value to others is certainly diminished. However, many important goods, like TV and radio signals, police and fire protection, parks, roads, and street lights, fall into the realm of public goods. They may not all be perfect examples, as roads can be blocked to prevent entry and parks can fill up, but they share the non-rival and nonexcludable characteristics at least up to a point.

Scenario

Your instructor has credited your fictional bank account with $10 worth of funny money. This will buy you nothing, but it gives you pleasure just knowing that you have it (especially if you have more than your neighbor). Being a kind and generous person, your instructor has agreed to double any amount of money that is invested in his or her "doubling pool" and divide this doubled amount among everyone in the class. All students receive an equal share of the doubled pool regardless of their investment or lack thereof. You can invest any amount from 0 to $10 (no change please) to be doubled. Record the amount you want to invest on the small investment recording slip (a.k.a., scrap paper) provided by your instructor and hand it in at the designated time. Your instructor will add up all of the investments, double them, and divide that amount by the number of students in the class. If a total of $150 is invested and there are 20 students in the class, the $150 becomes $300 when doubled and this is divided among 20 students to obtain the $15 share for each student. Those who invested $10 will end up with a total of $15. Those who invested nothing will get $15 to add to the $10 they kept for a total of $25. If everyone invested $10, everyone would end up with $20. You may discuss contributions with your classmates prior to making your investment decisions, but the actual investment amounts will be collected anonymously so that no one knows the strategy of any other particular person.

Reflections

(Please answer these questions *after* completing the classroom experiment.)

1. What strategy for the class would maximize the total amount of money received by each student?

2. Did you follow that strategy? If not, why?

3. Did your class experience a free-rider problem, meaning that students attempted to benefit from the investments of others without contributing their fair share?

4. Other than the goods mentioned in the description of this experiment, list at least two other goods that might face similar free-rider problems when people try to collect money to fund them in real life.

5. What role could government play in providing the socially optimal quantity of public goods while avoiding the free-rider problem?

6. Some people do make voluntary donations to help fund public or nearly public goods like National Public Radio, the Public Broadcasting System, churches, and community centers. What could explain this behavior?

Afterthoughts

Those trying to collect contributions to pay for public goods, like neighborhood groups collecting for a central flower display, often experience free-rider problems because citizens can benefit from the public good whether or not they contribute. Similarly, investment in this experiment's doubling pool invited free riding. By not investing, students obtained the benefits from others' investments while holding on to their own money. In both cases, even though the benefits to society exceed the cost of investment, each person's selfish incentive is to contribute nothing. The outcome is a form of market failure that results in less than the socially optimal quantity of these goods being produced and consumed. Note that unlike other types of goods, since many people can benefit from the *same* unit of a public good, the additional or "marginal" benefit from one more unit of a public good is determined by adding up the marginal benefit to each member of society who would benefit from that unit.

Classroom Experiment 7.B

Externality Experiment: The Ecomedy Club

Time Required: *15-20 minutes*

Materials Required: *2–3 random books, identical or not*

10 knock-knock jokes (provided by instructor)

Purpose: *To demonstrate negative externalities and link the reality with the theory.*

Level of Difficulty: *moderate. Comedians should perform cost-benefit analysis when deciding how many jokes to purchase and "memorizers" are asked to memorize a few lines of text.*

Textbook Coverage of Underlying Topics:
Arnold Ch. 30, McConnell/Brue Ch. 30, Mankiw Ch. 10, Colander Ch. 18, McEachern Ch. 17, Baumol/Blinder Ch. 20

Introduction

Externalities are effects felt beyond those whose decisions or actions cause the effects. Externalities are an important source of market failure that we experience every day, although we may not be aware of it. Is the barking of your neighbor's dog a nuisance? Do you love it when your fraternity brother bakes bread, which fills the house with a wonderful aroma? In these situations, you are experiencing externalities. This activity provides insight into externalities, and will allow you to feel and graph private and social costs, identify utility-maximizing and socially optimal consumption levels, and prescribe appropriate remedies.

Scenario

This experiment involves three independent producers of human capital (*memorizers*) and two joint consumers of humor (*comedians*). The comedians should be seated on opposite sides of the room, with the memorizers seated roughly in the middle. The memorizers' goal is to memorize as many consecutive words in a randomly selected sentence as they can in 30 seconds. The hypothetical payoff for the human capital the memorizers attain (perhaps the ability to score well on exams or impress important people) is worth $3 per word memorized. In case you are selected as a memorizer, practice memorizing words for 30 seconds once or twice.

For the comedians, the marginal cost of each joke is $5 (this represents the cost of buying each joke from the writer). In this Ecomedy Club, there is diminishing marginal utility from humor. The marginal utility from the first 10 jokes is as follows:

JOKE	MU (IN DOLLARS)
1	10
2	9
3	8
4	7
5	6
6	5
7	4
8	3
9	2
10	1

With silence in the room, the memorizers will open their books to a random page and see how many consecutive words they can memorize in 30 seconds. Your instructor will keep the time, and when it is up, your instructor will measure and record the human capital production by asking each memorizer to recite his or her words as the instructor looks at the section studied in the book.

The above step is repeated, but this time the joke tellers create their humor at the same time. That is, one comedian holds the joke sheet (provided by your instructor) and calls out to the comedian on the other side of the room, "Knock knock . . . ." The other comedian gives the appropriate responses.

Reflections

(Please answer these questions *after* completing the classroom experiment.)

1. Acting on their own self-interests, how many jokes should the comedians have told?

2. In what ways did comedy consumption create effects felt beyond or "external to" the consumers of comedy?

3. Did the comedians take this into account when deciding how many jokes to tell?

4. Consider the memorizer whose word count dropped by neither the most nor the least. What was the effect of joke-telling on his or her human capital production? In other words, what was the total external cost for the median memorizer?

5. Assuming that each joke eliminated the same amount of memorization (so that the marginal external cost and the average external cost are the same), what was the marginal external cost in dollars; that is, the additional external cost per joke for the median memorizer?

6. From a societal standpoint, which considers both private and external costs (to the median memorizer), how many jokes should have been told?

7. Graph the private marginal cost, social marginal cost, and marginal utility. Indicate the private and social optimums.

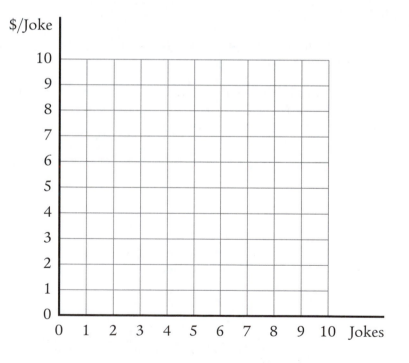

8. In what situations do we face similar problems with negative externalities in the real world?

9. How could we reduce or prevent the over-consumption of goods that create negative externalities?

Afterthoughts

You have now witnessed the creation of externalities and the concurrent separation of private marginal cost and social marginal cost caused by that pesky marginal external cost. Externalities are everywhere, and our markets are inefficient in their presence. The resulting market failure beckons for solutions, which can include taxes, subsidies, and quotas. That is one of the important roles of government. The catch is that we need well-informed policy makers and voters to administer these corrective measures in such a way that they don't cause more harm than good. That is one of the important roles of education. Thanks for taking part.

Classroom Experiment 7.C

Tragedy of the Commons Experiment: Where the Moose Roam

Time Required: *20 minutes*	**Level of Difficulty:** *low to moderate. Players make decisions under uncertainty.*
Materials Required: *1 herd of moose (supplied by your instructor, for those not in the North)*	**Textbook Coverage of Underlying Topics:** *Arnold Ch. 30,*
Purpose: *To place students into the context of an open-access resource and allow them to feel the incentives provided by differing solutions.*	*McConnell/Brue Ch. 30, Mankiw Ch. 11, Colander Ch. 18, McEachern Ch. 17, Baumol/Blinder Ch. 20*

Introduction

As your economics course continues, you will learn not only the workings of markets, but the critical importance of various components of our economic system. This activity will shed light on the roles of government and property rights in reconciling the supply and demand of exploitable resources.

Scenario

You are a meat and fur trader in the rugged North. As you hunt moose, you are aware of the following facts:

- Each hunting season lasts 30 seconds.

- If there are fewer than eight moose, reproduction will not occur (for lack of genetic and gender diversity).

- Given that there are eight moose, the number of moose will double after each hunting season. That is, if 10 moose remain after a hunting season, there will be 20 moose the next hunting season.

- When hunting, you care only about the number of moose and not about age or location.

- Despite the fact that moose appear cute and friendly, so are your spouse and child, and this is the only means by which to feed and clothe your wife and child. Thus, you want to maximize your "harvest."

- Finally, you plan to be around for many more periods, and you do not know how many more hunting seasons remain.

Other aspects of the scenario will change over the periods, as indicated by your instructor. In each of the periods, examine your interests and incentives and then make the "best" choice in regard to your moose harvest.

Reflections

(Please answer these questions *after* completing the classroom experiment.)

1. What is the role of property rights in the allocation of moose?

2. Great philosophers like John Locke have argued that government is necessary in providing for property ownership. Give specific examples of the roles government plays in assigning and enforcing property rights.

3. Are there places on your school's campus that suffer from the tragedy of the commons—in other words, the lack of well-defined property rights?

4. Are there existing problems in society that could be solved if only we could better assign property rights? If so, provide some examples.

Afterthoughts

Moose hunting aside, the lesson you just learned applies to everything from radio waves to the open sea. Ownership of the former has been assigned, much like property rights, to prevent broadcasters from trampling upon each other's frequencies. The oceans are harder to monitor, not to mention the difficulty of finding agreement over property rights among the many nations bordering the sea. As our experiment would predict, private land, livestock, and radio wave frequencies are well cared for, while problems with excess pollution and overhunting in open-access areas persist.

Problem Set 7.1

Tax Incidence

Local authorities view the production of "Famous Economist Trading Cards" as a threat to the welfare of Econville's citizenry. To limit risk exposure, they levy a tax on the manufacture of these cards in hopes that it will discourage consumption. The following graph demonstrates the supply and demand for "Famous Economist Trading Cards," taking into account the private cost and benefit of their production.

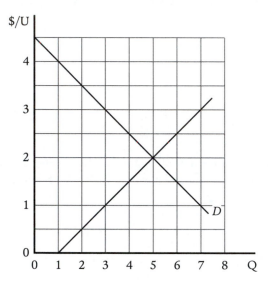

1. Identify the equilibrium price and quantity of "Famous Economist Trading Cards."

2. On the graph, demonstrate the effect of imposing a $1.00 per card tax on the production of the cards.

3. Identify the new price that consumers pay and the price producers receive after paying the tax.

4. Compare your answers to 1 and 3 above, and comment on who bears the burden (or incidence) of this tax.

5. Repeat questions 1–4 for the following graphs.

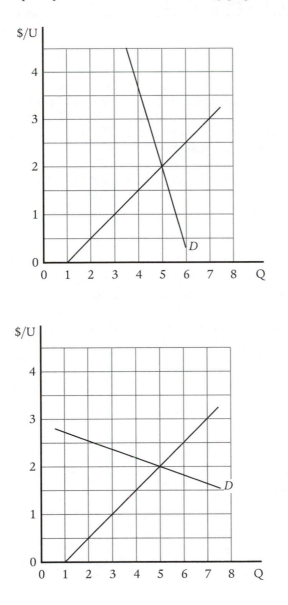

6. What can you conclude about the relationship between tax incidence and the demand for the good being taxed?

Problem Set 7.2

Progressivity

In the country of Econville, there are four states: Microland, Macroland, Tradeland, and Consumerland. Each of these states has its own state tax system, and the country of Econville has a value added tax of 10 percent on the purchase of all goods sold in the country. In the table below are the taxes for each of the states.

INCOME	MICROLAND TAX	MACROLAND TAX	TRADELAND TAX	CONSUMERLAND TAX
$10,000	$1,000	$1,000	$1,000	$1,000
$20,000	$1,000	$2,000	$1,250	$2,500
$30,000	$1,000	$3,000	$1,500	$4,250
$40,000	$1,000	$4,000	$1,750	$6,500
$50,000	$1,000	$5,000	$2,000	$9,500

1. Classify the tax structures of each of the states as being either progressive, proportional, or regressive.

2. Explain in each case how you were able to classify the tax system of each state.

3. Classify Econville's value added tax and explain how you made that determination.

Problem Set 7.3

Classifying Taxes

Indicate whether the following taxes are based on the ability-to-pay principle of taxation or the benefits-received principle of taxation and whether they are progressive, proportional, or regressive.

		ABILITY-TO-PAY OR BENEFITS-RECEIVED	PROGRESSIVE, PROPORTIONAL, OR REGRESSIVE
1.	A flat-rate income tax	_____	_____
2.	A set fee to use a toll road	_____	_____
3.	The present federal income tax	_____	_____
4.	A sales tax	_____	_____
5.	The present social security tax	_____	_____
6.	A set amount of money to be paid in tax by everyone	_____	_____

Problem Set 7.4

Positive Externalities

Phillipo Epstein, a standout student at Buchanan High School, decided to produce a fireworks show to honor the writing of the *Wealth of Nations*. Phillipo would hire a pyrotechnic firm to actually produce the fireworks, and he would charge admission to the event. He made arrangements to rent the field hockey stadium at Buchanan High School to hold the large crowd he expected to attend. The following graph shows the private cost and private benefit that Phillipo anticipated for the fireworks show. Based on this information, he decided to charge an admission price of $10 per person. On the actual night of the show, Phillipo was shocked and horrified to find out that many of the expected customers simply watched the show from outside of the stadium and did not pay the admission fee. After the show, he added up the gate receipts and recalculated demand. The new demand was 50 percent as much as Phillipo's original estimate.

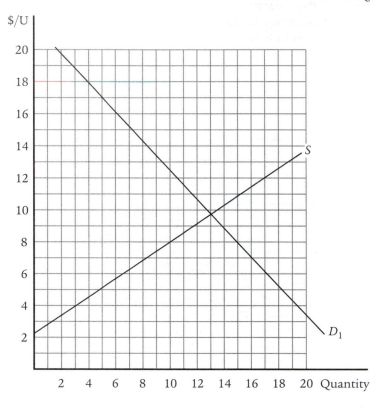

1. Identify the equilibrium price and quantity for the fireworks show that Phillipo Epstein had originally anticipated.

2. Calculate the new demand and plot it on the graph.

3. Identify the new quantity demanded at $10 per ticket.

4. If the original demand is the "real" demand for fireworks shows, which was tempered by the ability to watch the show from outside the stadium, what can you conclude about the likelihood of financial success for events like the fireworks show to celebrate the writing of the *Wealth of Nations*?

5. What is the economic problem associated with the presence of significant positive externalities?

6. Explain one market-based solution that would correct for this misallocation of resources.

7. What are some other examples of activities that create positive externalities? Are these activities subsidized, and if not, do you think they should be?

Problem Set 7.5

Negative Externalities

A company has decided to locate its new textbook manufacturing plant on the local river. Effluent from the production process is released into the river. When questioned about this practice, the company responded that it is cheaper to release waste into the river than to have it hauled away. In the weeks that followed, much discussion took place and eventually the local authorities decided to impose a $25 per unit tax on this company.

The following graph shows the private cost and private benefit of the plant.

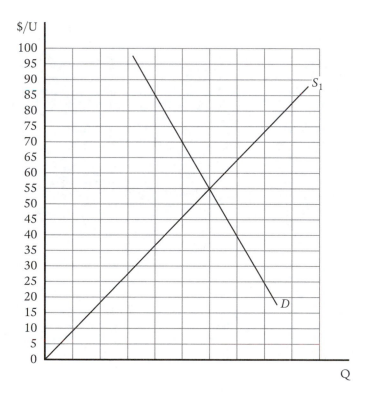

1. Identify the equilibrium price and quantity for textbooks from the plant.

2. Calculate the new supply (with the imposition of the tax) and plot it on the above graph.

3. Identify the new quantity demanded.

4. If it is true that the original supply curve depicts the private cost of producing textbooks given the ability to release effluent into the river and that the new supply curve (including the tax) depicts the social cost of producing textbooks, what cost do people not associated with the production or consumption of textbooks pay per textbook produced?

5. What is the resource allocation problem associated with the presence of significant negative externalities?

6. Explain one market-based solution that would correct for this misallocation of resources.

7. What are some other examples of activities that create negative externalities? How would you suggest that we correct for the resulting market failure?

Problem Set 7.6

Congested Parks—A Pricing Dilemma

This reading provides a worthwhile overview of supply, demand, and efficiency issues in the context of environmental affairs and serves as the basis for the problems that follow. Some sections involve economic concepts that you have not yet covered and serve to foreshadow and motivate upcoming material.

Our national parks, along with many state and local recreation areas, strain to accommodate ever-increasing numbers of visitors. It is easy to conclude that these congestion difficulties justify the creation of new public parks and expansion of outdoor recreation facilities in existing parks. Additions to supply would seem appropriate, considering the rising demand. Yet, the apparently inadequate capacities of various public parks may reflect something other than a lag in the adjustment of supply to growing demand. Governments may be distorting the recreation market by charging too little for the recreational use of public parks. Such an improper pricing practice could lead to the misallocation of resources. Some groups would benefit—perhaps those that are not intended to—at the expense of others. Economic analysis helps to show the nature and probable consequences of the park crowding problems.

When Demand Crowds Supply

Overflowing visitation at a public park provides a textbook display of a shortage. Park crowding means insufficient park space—or types of park space, such as camping space, driving space, fishing space, etc.—to satisfy outdoor recreationists. They want more. Their wants, however, depend directly on what they must pay. The existence of a shortage says only that the quantity demanded exceeds the quantity supplied at the going price. Excessive park crowding, therefore, reflects a park entry or a park privilege fee that is below the one that equates the amount of park space consumers want to the amount available.

Figure 1 shows a set of demand and supply relationships for camping spaces in a hypothetical public park. Demand curve D_1 shows that the lower the price, the larger the number of identical park camping spaces desired on an average summer day. Vertical line S_1 indicates the number of camping spaces in the park, assumed to be an invariable quantity in the short run. Suppose park officials set the camping fee at $2. Quantity demanded (60 spaces) exceeds quantity supplied (20 spaces), so a shortage of 40 spaces prevails at that price.

What happens to the 40 camping families whom the park cannot accommodate? Those who can return home may disappointedly do so. Others may not show up, having heard about or previously experienced the shortage. Still others may try to squeeze and shoehorn into the camping area or pitch their tents in unauthorized

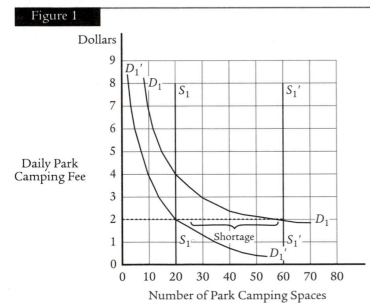

Figure 1

Dollars / Daily Park Camping Fee (vertical axis)
Number of Park Camping Spaces (horizontal axis)

Adapted from: Monthly Review, St. Louis Federal Reserve, Dan M. Bechter.

areas of the park. Some may find other public or private places to camp nearby. The remainder may stay in motels, sleep along the road, or drive all night.

As can be seen, selling a good or service below the market-clearing price—where demand equals supply, or $4, in the example—simply requires other forms of rationing or adjustment, such as first come, first served, which places a premium on arrival time. Some of these adaptations, in effect, increase the cost of the outdoor recreation experience. They make the consumer spend extra time and money for participation in the leisure activity. Other adjustments, such as crowding into available space, make outdoor recreation less fun.

The shortage shown in Figure 1—or any market shortage for that matter—can be reduced by (a) increasing price; (b) increasing supply; (c) decreasing demand; or (d) a combination of the preceding. Before considering these solutions, consider a part of what is going on outside the park.

Figure 2 shows another set of supply and demand curves—those for camping spaces on private land near the hypothetical public park. Currently, entrepreneurs are making 18 such spaces available and charging the market price of $2.50. Note that quantity demanded equals quantity supplied at this price; there is no shortage here. On a day of normal demand, everyone who wants to camp in a private area can do so. Some of the demand for private camping space depends, of course, on overflow from the public park. Assuming that campers prefer locations within the park to those outside, it might seem strange that some are willing to pay the extra half dollar charged by private campgrounds. It must be remembered, however, that the park cannot satisfy demand at $2. Also, note that a sizable portion of the left tail of demand curve D_1 in Figure 1 lies above the $4 price line, indicating that several campers are willing to pay more than this amount for places inside the park. Some of these people certainly would be willing to locate outside for less when the park is full.

Now, consider each of the solutions to the shortage of public park camping spaces. Suppose first that the park authorities raise their camping fee to $4. We see in Figure 1 that the shortage immediately disappears. Everyone wanting a space within the park at this price finds one, because quantity demanded declines from 60 to 20 spaces. In addition, because of the increase in the park's camping fee, more people will decide in favor of the less expensive private facilities. Demand curve D_2 for private camping spaces (Figure 2) will shift over to D_2'. For a while, there will be a shortage of private camping spaces, and campground owners may raise their prices. Eventually they will expand, or new private campgrounds will open. This is what curve S_1' shows—the number of camping spaces private landowners will supply, given the opportunity to adjust to various prices. As we see, the market price settles at $3 a space, where quantity demanded equals quantity supplied at 29 spaces. (S_2' slopes upward to the right, showing that costs per space increase as space is increased.) Furthermore, the market for motel rooms, among other related markets, will be affected.

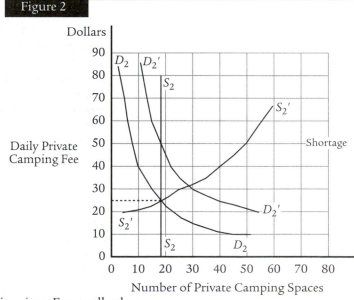

Figure 2

Dollars

Daily Private Camping Fee

Number of Private Camping Spaces

Suppose that instead of increasing price, the park officials increase the number of camping spaces from 20 to 60, shifting supply out to S_1' in Figure 1. Again, the shortage disappears. As a result, however, the private campgrounds receive less business. (In Figure 2, D_2 shifts left—not shown.) The markets for hotels among other substitutes and complements are affected, too.

Instead of increasing the number or price of camping spaces in the existing park, authorities could alleviate the crowding problem by reducing the demand for these spaces. (D_1 would shift left to D_1' in Figure 1.) They could achieve this by allowing the quality of the park facilities to decrease, opening additional parks, or subsidizing private campgrounds to lower their costs and encourage their expansion and improvement.

Each of these alternatives affects the outdoor recreation market differently. If camping conditions in the public park are allowed to deteriorate, for example, the demand for private campground spaces in the vicinity might rise as the desirability of these private areas increases relative to those in the park. On the other hand, the region may become less attractive as an outdoor recreation area, especially if the whole park deteriorates, and private enterprise also may suffer declines in demand. Creating more public parks or subsidizing private outdoor recreation areas in the region should decrease demand for space in individual parks, at least in the short run. It could also make the whole area more attractive as a recreation destination and, thereby, increase demand for all of the parks in the long run.

How Many People? How Much per Person?

Since undue crowding caused by an economic shortage can be eliminated by increasing the price, one wonders why this quick and obvious solution is not chosen. Alternatively, when "idle" space seems plentiful in the park, why not develop it for the more intensive recreational purposes that consumers want? Clearly, certain obstacles must be barring the wholesale use of these prescriptions. Indeed, several less apparent economic considerations make it difficult to determine the desirable amount of park use. Still other socioeconomic factors affect decisions of how to best allocate this use among outdoor recreationists.

Principles of Private Pricing

As a starting point, it proves helpful to think of how a public park would be managed if it were a privately owned enterprise. Microeconomic analysis proceeds from the axiom that an individual economic unit behaves in ways that it believes to be in its own self-interest. The theory of the firm treats profits as a measure of self-interest, and economists have found that the simple assumption that business enterprises act to maximize profits explains much of firm behavior. Assume that this objective—profit maximization—guides the park managers. Under such an assumption, what can one expect?

The owners may conclude that their land and water holdings would yield higher profits if used for purposes other than, or in addition to, outdoor recreation. With profit maximization as their goal, they may choose to turn the park into a farm, a strip mine, an oil field, or a residential area. Is this bad? Maybe, but the free country, free market philosophy argues that consumers, with their dollar votes, should direct the use of resources. In an idealized economic system, higher profit levels serve to stimulate production of those goods and services that society wants most. However, market imperfections such as its inability to incorporate external pollution costs and an excessive discounting of the value of resources to future generations leave our economy well shy of this idealized state. Consequently, profit signals cannot always be relied on to allocate resources in society's best interest, not to mention the best interest of other living things.

In the absence of such shortcomings, the most profitable use of resources would presumably be the most economically desirable. Thus, if private interests would operate resources differently from the government, the public use may have a questionable economic basis. The government should be able to defend its choice of uses by establishing the presence of considerations not fully reflected in profits and by showing that the inclusion of these considerations favors using the resources in a less profitable manner. Otherwise—putting this back into context—if the government cannot show that the net economic benefits of a public park at least equal those society receives by allowing the same area of land and water to be operated for the top competing purpose, the park cannot be justified.

Note that in choosing from alternative uses of resources, it is wrong to say that "other factors besides economics must be considered." Economics is the study of choices among competing alternatives. When making such choices, it is appropriate *within* economic analysis to consider all of the relevant factors, whether or not they involve money. The trick is to identify and include all of the relevant economic considerations, both current and future, when calculating benefits and costs. Confusion arises because many people commonly, but incorrectly, use the word "economics" as if it were synonymous with "profits" or "private enterprise." For example, a television special about a national park reported that the reconsideration of plans for a new airport represented a victory for conservation over economics. That was not the case. It represented a reassessment of the net benefits from building the airport. Society decided that it would be worse off—all things considered—with the airport, and so the decision not to build it was a wise choice in terms of both economics and conservation.

Returning to the question of pricing, suppose that businessmen do operate the parkland as an outdoor recreation area. To keep things simple, let the rental of camping spaces be the park's sole market activity. The profit maximizing owners will need to know (a) the demand for their camping spaces and (b) the amount it costs them to supply varying numbers of camping spaces.

Complexities appear quickly. The relationship between price and quantity demanded is complicated by the fact that the quality of the product depends on the number of people buying it. Up to a point, the representative camper may enjoy the camping experience more as the number of other campers in the park increases. He likes their company. Eventually, however, increases in the number of campers reduce the camper's total satisfaction. He dislikes crowding. Assuming the quality of camping first rises and then falls with the number of campers, the amount the camper is willing to pay rises then falls as well (Figure 3).

It is apparent that demand depends implicitly on supply. In the short run, a fixed amount of parkland cannot supply various

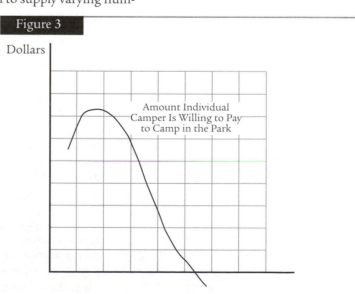

Figure 3

Dollars

Amount Individual Camper Is Willing to Pay to Camp in the Park

Number of Campers in the Park

quantities of constant-quality camping spaces. Campers want more than just a place to sleep. They also want open, natural spaces around them. When more camping spaces are supplied, less open space remains. Because of the crowding phenomenon, quantity demanded may become unresponsive to reductions in price once certain degrees of congestion are reached. Rational profit-maximizing park owners would never reduce price under such circumstances.

In their cost calculation, the park owners will allow for upkeep. As more camping spaces are rented, the cost of maintaining each additional space may decline as certain economies are realized. On the other hand, the least expensive ways of supplying camping spaces may be exhausted early. Also, as the number of camping spaces grows, the cost of maintaining the quality (of the decreased quantity) of open space might increase, perhaps dramatically, as certain critical levels of camping pressure are reached. For example, the park's wildlife—a prime attraction to campers—may cease to reproduce without sufficient space and seclusion.

Taking all internal cost and demand considerations into account, owners maximize profits by choosing price and quantity such that further reductions in price would increase revenues from camping space rentals by less than the cost of supplying these additional spaces.

Principles of Public Pricing

Parks often possess unique features and are located unequal distances from the homes of their visitors. This product differentiation implies that each park faces a downward-sloping demand curve. Under such monopolistically competitive conditions, owners must reduce prices on all spaces in order to rent more spaces, and thus, the additional or marginal revenue from renting one more camping space is less than the price at which it is rented. Profits decline with increased "sales" once marginal cost exceeds marginal revenue, and therefore, profits are below their maximum at the higher quantity where price equals marginal cost. For the economy as a whole, economic efficiency requires that resources be used until the marginal social benefit of each resulting good or service equals its marginal social cost. If all of society's costs of park use are borne by the park owners, and if all of society's benefits of park use are received by the park visitors, it follows that the profit-maximizing price will limit park use more than is desirable. Private owners will stop short of the point where the resource cost of supplying that last camping space exactly equals what society is willing to pay for it.

This leads directly to the obvious but important corollary: Under conditions of monopolistic competition where all costs and benefits of park use are internal (that is, felt by those who create the costs and benefits), the socially optimal amount of park congestion exceeds that which would be permitted by unregulated private enterprise. People may complain of crowded conditions in a public park, but that in itself does not justify limits on visitation. So long as the discomforts of crowding are internalized—that is, so long as visitors would accept them in exchange for the correspondingly low prices—the park visitor (assuming she or he fully anticipates the situation) has no economic grounds for complaint.

People who do not visit a park may benefit from those who do. Juvenile delinquency, for example, may be reduced by providing city park and recreation areas. These external benefits might justify a subsidy—a payment to those who use the park. It sounds strange, but why not? If, for example, it is found that children who participate in little league baseball are less likely to get sick, less likely to turn to crime, and less likely to go on welfare, might it not make sense to expand such programs even if it requires giving the participants some monetary inducement? Nonvisitors also may benefit from a park's provision of natural habitat for wildlife, its protection of rare plants and animals, and its preservation of unique natural and historical areas. Birds that nest in a park, for example, fly, feed, and sing far outside its boundaries. Benefits are sometimes less obvious. Relatively few people have ever seen a whooping crane, but millions derive pleasure from reading and hearing about its fight for survival. Conceivably, therefore, society's interest could be served by subsidizing park crowds if not more parks.

On the other hand, the benefits that nonvisitors receive may be *inversely* related to the number of park visitors. The more people who drive to the park, for example, the more highway congestion and air pollution for everyone. Park wildlife can damage crops and otherwise increase the cost of farming and ranching. As already noted, greater visitor pressure can reduce park quality. To the extent that added visitation decreases the benefits that nonvisitors get from the park, park visits impose a cost on society. In the camping space example, external benefits of nonuse increase the economically appropriate price and decrease the desirable level of camping. If government officials ignore these external costs and benefits in their pricing of park services, society will not be best served.

A Pricing Dilemma

The theory of optimal pricing is, of course, far easier than its practice. It is one thing to say that all costs and benefits should be identified and measured, another to figure out how. These difficulties are important but are not the topic of concern here. Rather, this section focuses on an obstacle that keeps park officials from charging the economically appropriate price for park use even when that price is known—public opinion.

The conditions reported at some popular public parks do not suggest an equilibrium in quantity demanded and quantity supplied. True, as shown earlier in this article, congestion is sometimes economically desirable and can be expected to cause complaints of crowding. But when people are turned away and when overuse threatens the park's survival, something must be out of kilter. Park authorities seem to be both encouraging visitation with low fees and discouraging visitation by not adequately expanding recreation facilities and by otherwise limiting—in nonprice fashions—the activities of the visitors.

Public opinion forces this strange behavior. In theory, at least, economists can usually fit public opinion into the pricing system by translating it into the dollar values that society places on the activities in question, like saving the bald eagle or cleaning up a polluted river. In this case, however, public opinion is against the pricing system. People strongly resist public park fees and the use of these fees to allocate park use. Americans apparently feel that public parks are theirs to use free of charge (or at nominal cost) as a right of part ownership. Strangely, they do not seem to feel this way about the nation's highways (we have gasoline taxes as well as turnpike tolls). On highways too, however, improper pricing results in crowded conditions.

Related to the ownership argument is the redistributive argument that entry fees would have to be raised substantially to adequately limit visitation and that this would discriminate against the poor. It might seem unlikely that the demand for a one-day park visit would be inelastic (meaning that price would have to go up by a lot to cause visitation to go down even by a little), but this may well be the case for parks like

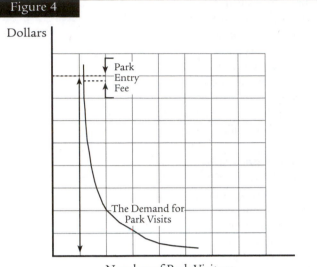

| Figure 4 |

Dollars

Park Entry Fee

The Demand for Park Visits

Number of Park Visitors

Yellowstone, because such large increases in entry fees may amount to relatively small percentage increases in the total cost of the park visit (Figure 4).

Until attitudes change, government officials face great resistance to increases in public park entry and use fees. Perhaps much of this resistance would decrease if proper pricing methods were used. Accelerating park deterioration and other costs of excessive crowding certainly call for changes in the pricing of park recreation. Paradoxically, governments appear to be working in the wrong direction. New highways to parks, for example, lower the time and cost of a visit. The Golden Eagle Passport—a $50 annual permit that admits the purchaser and accompanying passengers to more than 3,000 designated federal outdoor recreation areas—encourages more visitation.

Some groups, besides visitors, obviously benefit from park subsidies. Vested interests point to the regional activity generated by park use. Owners and employees of lodging places, restaurants, bait and tackle stores, and many other kinds of businesses and concessions do not want to give up what is actually a subsidy to them. They reason that if parks increase fees, the demand for the complementary goods and services they sell will decline. Manufacturers of boats, automobiles, and other outdoor recreation equipment also benefit from the subsidization of park use.

Other groups suffer. It can be argued that the subsidization of park recreation reduces the demand for movies, bowling, and other activities that consumers consider substitutes. Ronald F. Lee writes ". . . for most people, there is no substitute for a visit to a national park."[1] A visit to a national park may be a unique experience, but that does not mean it has no substitutes. Most Americans already substitute other things—staying home, for example—for national park visits. And if the price of visiting national parks is increased, even more people will substitute other leisure activities.

Further Complexities and Ideas

Most public parks of any size supply several different types of outdoor recreation. Many of these compete with one another for available park space. One example of this has already been given: Open space competes with park use. But water skiing competes with fishing, picnicking with camping, and so on. A park contains, therefore, several submarkets, and as such it can supply any one of many different types of park use mixes. Some activities use more resources than others, and these should be priced higher. In practice, it may be extremely difficult and expensive to collect for each activity engaged in by a park visitor, but it might be possible to approximate his cost by charging him on the basis of the time he spends in the park and the equipment he takes in. Perhaps simply multiplying time by total vehicle weight by a price for a standard "user unit" would do the job. This would (1) discourage long stays, (2) discourage autos, campers, boats, and other heavy equipment, and (3) permit a relatively low entry price for visitors willing to travel light within the park

[1]*Public Use of the National Park System, 1872–2000* (Washington: Department of the Interior, National Park Service, U.S. Government Printing, Office, 1968), p. 87.

and willing to stay only a short period. Some parks currently do not permit visitors to stay an indefinite periods of time. This is consistent with the philosophy that it is better for society if five people spend one day in the park than if one person spends five days. If this point of view is accepted, a fee rising *progressively* with length of stay is called for.

Seasonal park congestion could also be relieved by varying visitation fees by time of year. Although used to some extent, this method of pricing is largely untapped. The advance reservation idea probably favors certain groups over others, although it does have the advantage of guaranteeing space. Unfortunately, one likely outcome of a reservation system in situations where demand exceeds supply is a black market or scalper market in tickets. Why not use the pricing system directly instead of driving it underground?

The cost of park-type outdoor recreation must be borne by someone. This includes not only the direct operating costs but also the opportunity costs of the resources and the external costs net of external benefits. If the public wants this kind of activity enough to pay for it, private enterprises will have every incentive to provide such parks. And, of course, there are many private enterprises of this nature now in existence.

The question is whether we should trust private enterprise to correct for market failure better than public institutions and to preserve the natural beauty of the parks. Many park resources development decisions are irreversible, and the long-run consequences of a misguided short-run profit motive could be severe. On the other hand, public ownership does not guarantee development of resources in the long-run best interest of society either.

1. The Park Service faces the problem of overcrowding. There are three basic solutions. Use shifts or other changes in the graphs provided below to demonstrate each of these three solutions.

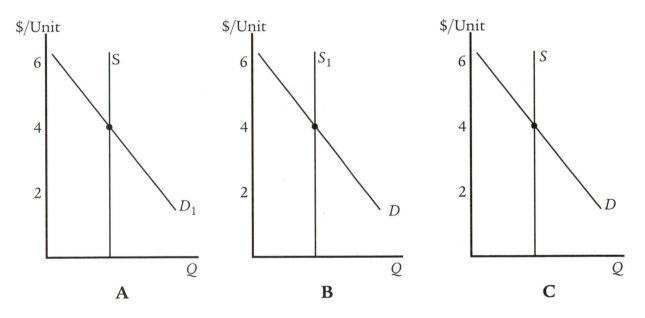

2. Which of the three solutions would you choose and why? (Be sure to list the advantage of your solution and the disadvantages of the others.)

3. Defend the statement that congestion is sometimes economically desirable.

4. Demonstrate the effect of letting hungry carnivorous grizzly bears roam free near the camping spaces in the park on the graph provided below.

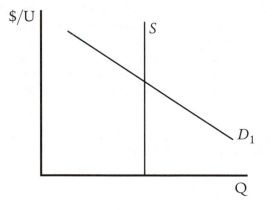

5. Demonstrate on the graph provided below the effect of increasing the speed limit to 80 mph and simultaneously lowering the price of a Golden Eagle park entry permit to $25.00.

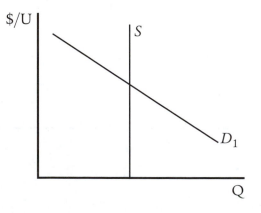

6. If the demand for park camping spaces tends to be inelastic, comment on the effectiveness of raising the price as a solution to overcrowding. How would your answer change if the demand for park camping were elastic?

7. Do you think the demand is inelastic or elastic? Why?

8. Do you agree or disagree that sometimes factors other than economics must be considered in cases like this?

Macroeconomic Indicators, Deficits, and Debt 8

Classroom Experiment 8.A

COLAs and Living Burger-to-Burger on Route 66

Time Required: *10–15 minutes*	**Level of Difficulty:** *low to moderate.*
Materials Required: *none*	
	Textbook Coverage of Underlying Topics:
Purpose: *To provide experience with cost of living adjustments and insight into the world of price variations.*	*Arnold Ch. 5, McConnell/Brue Ch. 7, Mankiw Ch. 30, Colander Ch. 22, McEachern Ch. 23, Baumol/Blinder Ch. 22*

Introduction

Entering the DeLorian in the movie *Back to the Future* would take you to a different time, when a hamburger at the same diner might cost a dime or $5, depending on the settings in the time machine. Entering a Dodge Neon today in reality and driving in any direction can generate the same results. A hamburger costs about a dime in Tijuana, Mexico, and over $5 at the Hard Rock Café in New York City. Although acquiring the Dodge is up to you, in this experiment you will take a virtual tour to explore the cost of living across the country, and contemplate the reasons for variations in the price of a hamburger.

Scenario

You and your class will take the Internet highway down old Route 66 from Chicago to Santa Monica, with a few side trips along the way. Your instructor will assign you one city on the route, and you are to estimate the cost of a hamburger there, starting with the fact that a burger costs a dollar in Amarillo, Texas. If you use a salary comparison Web site like http://www.homefair.com/calc/salcalc.html, simply say that your salary is $100,000 in Amarillo and ask it to tell you the equivalent amount in your assigned city. Divide by 100,000 to find the price of a burger. Alternatively, if you use cost-of-living index values for this calculation, you can apply the following formula:

$$\left(\frac{\text{Index Value for Your City}}{\text{Index Value for Amarillo}} \right) \times \$1.00 = \text{Price of Burger in Your City.}$$

After pricing burgers in your assigned city, try to find the highest and lowest prices in the United States. Perform your research prior to class, and fill in the following:

Your assigned city: _____

The price of a burger in your assigned city: _____

The most expensive city you could find (burger price and location): _____

The cheapest city you could find (burger price and location): _____

Reflections

(Please answer these questions *after* completing the classroom experiment.)

1. Why do prices change over time?

2. Why do prices differ in different places?

3. What prevents arbitrage between these cities? (Arbitrage is the process of buying at a low price and selling at a high price to gain riskless profit from unequal prices.)

4. Do the cross-country hamburger prices you came up with represent nominal or real values?

5. What would happen to the purchasing power of the money in your pocket if you moved from your assigned city to Amarillo?

Afterthoughts

Variations in the cost of living across locations make some places a real deal and other places money pits. Supply and demand drive the cost of living, and popular places tend to generate high demand for goods and correspondingly high prices. If you happen to like places that aren't so popular, you can live relatively high on the hog. For example, radio disc jockey Rick Dees owns hundreds of acres and a private golf course in central Kentucky. If he stayed in Los Angeles where his radio show is produced, the same investment in real estate would hardly buy him a miniature golf course.

Classroom Experiment 8.B

Budgetary Woes: A Balancing Act

Time Required: *30–45 minutes* **Materials Required:** *none* **Purpose:** *To provide insight into the challenges of budget allocation at the national level.* **Level of Difficulty:** *moderate*	**Textbook Coverage of Underlying Topics:** *Arnold Ch. 10,* *McConnell/Brue Ch. 18,* *Mankiw Ch. 26, Colander Ch. 31,* *McEachern Ch. 32,* *Baumol/Blinder Ch. 31*

Introduction

The primary purpose of this exercise is to introduce the general categories of government expenditure and the difficulty of allocating funds among these categories. There are 300 million Americans, 535 members of Congress, thousands of lobbyists, and an infinite number of ways to allocate the federal budget. All of this spells trouble when it comes time for the budget to balance. You will be working with only three of your fellow students, and the budget provided below has only 30 items. See how you do. You may find that your class could run government far more efficiently than the folks at it today, or you may gain an appreciation for the difficult economic dilemmas facing our representatives in Washington, D.C.

Scenario

You have $2 trillion that you and three other members of your government will allocate among the categories below. Typical expenditures and percentages are provided, first for spending on purchases and transfers and then for "tax expenditures" on various tax breaks. You may well want to change these allocations of the budget. Just as members of Congress have personal and political reasons to favor certain areas, you will have your own priorities. In addition to your preexisting preferences, suppose that you represent constituents with particular interests in several of these areas of spending. Notice that most of the spending categories below are labeled with a capital letter. The four people in your group, in alphabetical order according to your last names, have special interests in budget items A–F, G–M, N–S, and T–Z respectively. Upon reporting your group's results, you will receive a coveted invisible star and a silent clap for each 1 percent increase in spending on any of your special interests (as a percentage of the typical spending on those items), and you will lose one invisible star and silent clap for each 1 percent increase in spending on the special interests of your opponents. For example, suppose that one of your special interests is International Affairs and a special interest of someone else in the group is Transportation. If you agree on a budget that increases spending on International Affairs by 10 percent from 20 billion to 22 billion, and increases spending on Transportation by 5 percent from 40 billion to 42 billion, you get 10 – 5 = 5 invisible stars. The percentage change is found using the following formula:

$$\frac{(\text{New Expenditure} - \text{Typical Expenditure})}{(\text{Typical Expenditure})} \times 100.$$

Before or at the beginning of class (depending on your instructor's assignment), come up with your personal budget plan. In class you will be assigned to a group of four with whom to try to hash out an agreement on the budget. Although some of the recent U.S. leaders have overindulged, you are not permitted to spend more than you have. If you come to an agreement, write up your master plan and you will have the opportunity to post it or present it to the class.

SPENDING	TYPICAL PERCENT	TYPICAL EXPENDITURE (IN BILLIONS)	YOUR PLANNED DOLLARS (IN BILLIONS)
A. Military Spending	13.65	273	_____
B. Veterans and Military Retirement	3.35	67	_____
C. International Affairs (aid, State Department, etc.)	1	20	_____
D. General Science, Space, and Technology	0.9	18	_____
E. Non-Defense Energy Spending	0.25	5	_____
F. Natural Resources and Environment	1.1	22	_____
G. Agriculture	0.75	15	_____
H. Commerce and Housing Credit	–0.55	–11*	_____
I. Transportation	2	40	_____
J. Community and Regional Development	0.7	14	_____
K. Education, Training, Employment, and Social Services	2.85	57	_____
L. Non-Medicare Health Spending	5.8	116	_____
M. Medicare	7.9	158	_____
N. Non-Social Security Retirement and Unemployment	3.35	67	_____
O. Social Welfare Spending (housing assistance, nutrition programs, home energy assistance, etc.)	5.65	113	_____
P. Social Security	16.85	337	_____
Q. Administration of Justice (FBI, border enforcement, law enforcement, civil and criminal prosecution, etc.)	0.95	19	_____
R. General Government Administration (tax collection, legislative functions, general property and records management)	0.75	15	_____
Net Interest Payments	11.8	236	_____
Undistributed Offsetting Receipts (contributions to retirement programs, rents and royalties on continental shelf, etc.)	–2.05	–41	_____

*Housing credits are offset by receipts from loan guarantee programs.

Tax Expenditures	Typical Percent	Typical Expenditure (in billions)	Your Planned Dollars (in billions)
S. Corporate Tax Breaks	3.3	66	_____
T. Personal Business and Investment Benefits (capital gains, accelerated depreciation, other tax breaks)	3.65	73	_____
U. Pension and Retirement Plan Deductions	3.7	74	_____
V. Employer-Paid Health Insurance	2.7	54	_____
W. Itemized Deductions (mortgage interest, charitable contributions, medical expenses, state and local taxes, etc.)	4.15	83	
X. Earned Income Tax Credit	1.1	22	_____
Y. Untaxed Social Security Benefits	1.15	23	_____
Capital Gains on Homes	1.05	21	_____
Z. Medicare-related tax deductions	0.65	13	_____
Other Personal Tax Expenditures (fringe benefits, workers comp, child care credits, soldiers and veterans, etc.)	1.55	31	_____
Total	100	2000	_____

Reflections

(Please answer these questions *after* completing the classroom experiment.)

1. If you came to an agreement, what was the secret to your success? If you didn't, what were the major impediments?

2. How did your budget differ from the real thing? Would the changes you proposed go over well in Congress?

3. What surprised you the most about the typical budget?

4. In what significant ways do you think resources would be allocated differently if budgets were designed in the absence of pork-barrel politics?

Afterthoughts

There's an old saying that the two things one wouldn't want to see in the works are sausage and politics. Hopefully your negotiations weren't as ugly as the real thing, which has been known to shut down the government and occupy legislators for extended periods. For more practice at budget allocation, check out the excellent national budget simulation at http://www.budgetsim.org/nbs.

Problem Set 8.1

The Consumer Price Index

The only things the citizens of Econville eat and drink are root beer and chips. These two goods do not change in quality over time and are produced in the same way each year. Econville citizens consume these in a 3 cases of root beer per 2 bags of chips ratio. The prices of these two goods are listed below. Assume that each year consumers purchase 3 cases of root beer and 2 bags of chips.

	ROOT BEER	CHIPS
2002	$6.00	$1.00
2003	$6.50	$1.25
2004	$6.75	$1.40
2005	$7.15	$1.50

1. Calculate the total cost of what the typical consumer purchases in Econville in each of the years listed.

2. Using 2003 as the base year, calculate the consumer price index for each year.

3. Use the consumer price index figures from question 2 to calculate the rate of inflation from 2002 to 2003, 2003 to 2004, and 2004 to 2005.

Problem Set 8.2

Inflation

If inflation is anticipated to be 5 percent per year and actual inflation for that year turns out to be 7 percent, identify whether each of the following groups would be helped or hurt by this, or if the effort is indeterminate and why.

1. People who are living on fixed incomes.

2. Banks that have made long-term fixed rate loans.

3. People who have purchased bonds.

4. A person who has purchased real estate with a bank loan.

5. A recent college graduate with many loans to pay back.

6. People who have purchased stock.

7. Governments that have sold bonds.

8. Savers with open passbook accounts.

9. People who have purchased precious metals.

10. Wage earners who are members of a strong union.

Problem Set 8.3

Benchmarking Inflation

The following inflation figures were calculated using the Consumer Price Index for All Items (CPI-U) and represent the percent change from the previous year.

1960	1.7	1970	5.7	1980	13.5	1990	5.4	2000	3.6
1961	1.0	1971	4.4	1981	10.3	1991	4.2	2001	3.3
1962	1.0	1972	3.2	1982	6.2	1992	3.0	2002	1.1
1963	1.3	1973	6.2	1983	3.2	1993	3.0	2003	2.2
1964	1.3	1974	11.0	1984	4.3	1994	2.6	2004	2.9
1965	1.6	1975	9.1	1985	3.6	1995	2.8		
1966	2.9	1976	5.8	1986	1.9	1996	3.0		
1967	3.1	1977	6.5	1987	3.6	1997	2.3		
1968	4.2	1978	7.6	1988	4.1	1998	1.7		
1969	5.5	1979	11.3	1989	4.8	1999	1.9		

1. Plot the points for the percent change in the CPI for the decade of the 1960s on the graph below. Draw a horizontal line on your graph at the average level of inflation for the decade.

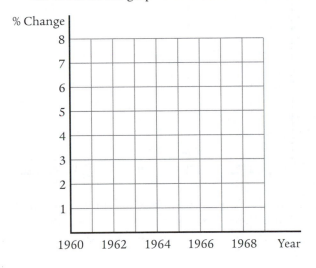

2. Plot the points for the percent change in the CPI for the decade of the 1970s on the graph to the right. Draw a horizontal line on your graph at the average level of inflation for the decade.

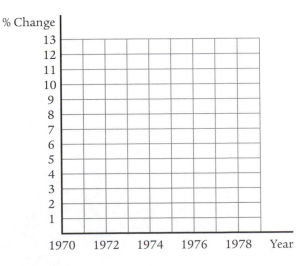

3. Plot the points for the percent change in the CPI for the decade of the 1980s on the graph below. Draw a horizontal line on your graph at the average level of inflation for the decade.

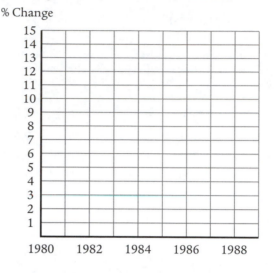

4. You guessed it—plot the points for the percent change in the CPI for the decade of the 1990s on the graph below. Draw a horizontal line on your graph at the average level of inflation for the decade.

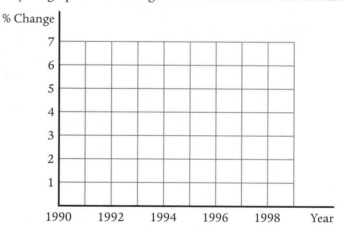

5. Average rates of inflation are considered estimates of the "natural rate of inflation" over decades (among other periods). Summarize your work in parts 1–4 by estimating the average rate of inflation for each decade.

6. Do a bit of research to find the annual percentage change in CPI-U since 2004, and create your own graph like the ones above for the years from 2000 to the present.

Problem Set 8.4

Gross Domestic Product

The following figures are available for an economy:

Consumer expenditures = $600

Business expenditures = $150

Government expenditures = $200

Imports = $75

Exports = $65

Transfer payments = $50

Depreciation = $25

1. Calculate gross domestic product for this economy.

2. The GDP figure that you calculated above is for year 1 and is comprised of:

    90 economics textbooks @ $10 each and

    40 economics workbooks @ $1 each.

    In year 2, this same economy produced:

    90 economics textbooks @ $15 each and

    40 economics workbooks @ $2 each.

    Calculate nominal GDP for year 1 and year 2.

3. Calculate the GDP deflator for this economy from year 1 to year 2 using the figures provided.

4. Calculate real GDP for year 2 for this economy.

5. Calculate real GDP if in 2005 nominal GDP is $1000 and the deflator is 200.

Problem Set 8.5

Economic Growth

The following historical data on the annual percent change in Real Gross Domestic Product come from the *Economic Report of the President.*

1960	2.5	1970	0.2	1980	–.2	1990	1.9	2000	3.7
1961	2.3	1971	3.4	1981	2.5	1991	–.2	2001	0.8
1962	6.1	1972	5.3	1982	–1.9	1992	3.3	2002	1.9
1963	4.4	1973	5.8	1983	4.5	1993	2.7	2003	3.0
1964	5.8	1974	–.5	1984	7.2	1994	4.0	2004	3.2*
1965	6.4	1975	–.2	1985	4.1	1995	2.5	*estimate	
1966	6.5	1976	5.3	1986	3.5	1996	3.7		
1967	2.5	1977	4.6	1987	3.4	1997	4.5		
1968	4.8	1978	5.6	1988	4.1	1998	4.2		
1969	3.1	1979	3.2	1989	3.5	1999	4.5		

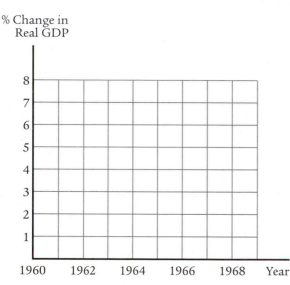

1. Plot the points for economic growth for the decade of the 1960s on the figure to the left. Draw a horizontal line on your graph so that half of the points are above the line and half of the points are below the line.

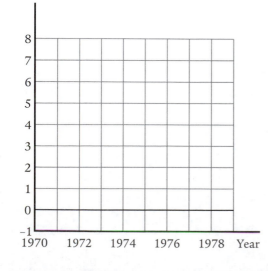

2. Plot the points for economic growth for the decade of the 1970s on the figure to the left. Draw a horizontal line on your graph so that half of the points are above the line and half of the points are below the line.

3. Plot the points for economic growth for the decade of the 1980s on the figure to the right. Draw a horizontal line on your graph so that half of the points are above the line and half of the points are below the line.

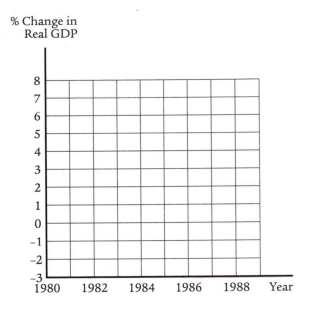

% Change in Real GDP

4. Plot the points for economic growth for the decade of the 1990s on the figure to the right. Draw a horizontal line on your graph so that half of the points are above the line and half of the points are below the line.

5. Summarize your answers to questions 1–4 by listing the average rate of economic growth for each decade.

6. What is the average or "natural" rate of economic growth" over the period from 1960 to the present?

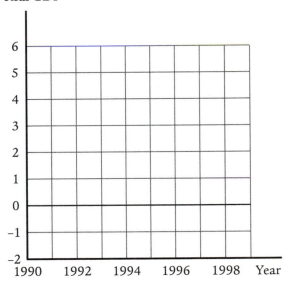

% Change in Real GDP

7. Find data on the percentage change in real GDP online and create your own graph like the ones above for the period from 2000 to the present.

Problem Set 8.6

Calculating the Unemployment Rate

The following formulas will be useful in answering the questions in this problem set:

Labor force = number of employed + number of unemployed

$$\text{Unemployment rate} = \left(\frac{\text{number of unemployed}}{\text{labor force}}\right) \times 100 \text{ percent}$$

$$\text{Labor-force participation rate} = \left(\frac{\text{labor force}}{\text{adult population}}\right) \times 100 \text{ percent}$$

Adult population	223 million
Employed	139 million
Unemployed	8 million
Not in labor force	76 million

1. Calculate the size of the labor force.

2. Calculate the unemployment rate.

3. Calculate the labor-force participation rate.

Problem Set 8.7

Types of Unemployment

Classify each of the following into the appropriate category of unemployment. Your choices are:

Frictional unemployment
Cyclical unemployment
Structural unemployment
Seasonal unemployment

1. An unemployed auto assembly line worker during a sales slump.

2. A snow plow driver during the summer.

3. A record player repairman who has not learned the latest laser disk player repair technology.

4. A computer programmer who quits his job to look for a job with better benefits.

5. A high school dropout with few skills who has been looking for a job unsuccessfully for weeks.

6. A recent business school graduate looking for her first job.

7. A person whose job has been automated out of existence.

8. A vendor who sells beer at major league baseball games during the winter months.

9. A welder who finds that robots have replaced most of the welding jobs on assembly lines.

10. A top salesman for a computer company who quit because he did not like his boss.

Problem Set 8.8

The Natural Rate of Unemployment

The following historical data on the Civilian Unemployment Rate in percentage terms come from the *Economic Report of the President*.

1950	5.3	1960	5.5	1970	4.9	1980	7.1	1990	5.6	2000	4.0
1951	3.3	1961	6.7	1971	5.9	1981	7.6	1991	6.8	2001	4.7
1952	3.0	1962	5.5	1972	5.6	1982	9.7	1992	7.5	2002	5.8
1953	2.9	1963	5.7	1973	4.9	1983	9.6	1993	6.9	2003	6.0
1954	5.5	1964	5.2	1974	5.6	1984	7.5	1994	6.1	2004	5.5*
1955	4.4	1965	4.5	1975	8.5	1985	7.2	1995	5.6	*estimate	
1956	4.1	1966	3.8	1976	7.7	1986	7.0	1996	5.4		
1957	4.3	1967	3.8	1977	7.1	1987	6.2	1997	4.9		
1958	6.8	1968	3.6	1978	6.1	1988	5.5	1998	4.5		
1959	5.5	1969	3.5	1979	5.8	1989	5.3	1999	4.2		

1. Plot the points for the unemployment rate for the decade of the 1950s on the figure to the right. Draw a horizontal line on your graph so that half of the points are above the line and half of the points are below the line.

2. Plot the points for the unemployment rate for the decade of the 1960s on the figure below. Draw a horizontal line on your graph so that half of the points are above the line and half of the points are below the line.

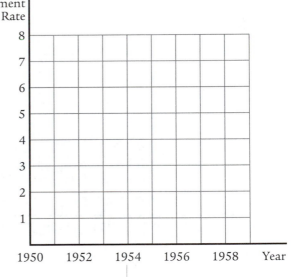

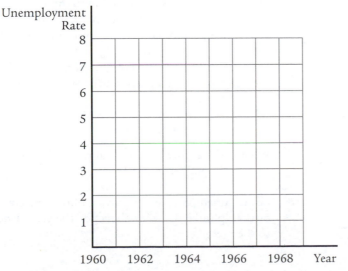

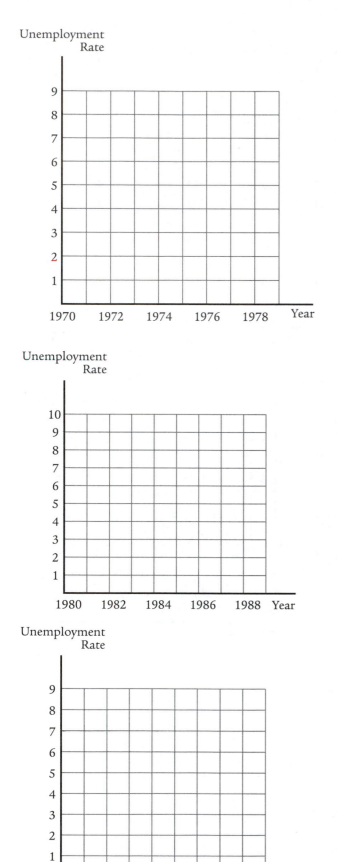

3. Plot the points for the unemployment rate for the decade of the 1970s on the figure to the left. Draw a horizontal line on your graph so that half of the points are above the line and half of the points are below the line.

4. Plot the points for the unemployment rate for the decade of the 1980s on the figure to the left. Draw a horizontal line on your graph so that half of the points are above the line and half of the points are below the line.

5. Plot the points for the unemployment rate for the decade of the 1990s on the figure to the left. Draw a horizontal line on your graph so that half of the points are above the line and half of the points are below the line.

6. Summarize your answers to questions 1–5 by listing the average rate of unemployment for each decade.

7. What is the average or "natural rate" of unemployment over the period from 1950 to the present?

8. Locate unemployment figures online and create your own graph like the ones above for the years from 2000 to the present.

Problem Set 8.9

Real vs. Nominal values

The following are box office receipts for the 50 highest grossing movies of all time (and two additional movies of special interest) as listed on http://www.movieweb.com. These values are in millions of actual (nominal) dollars, meaning that no adjustments have been made for inflation.

TOP ALL TIME HIGHEST GROSSING MOVIES
(Gross domestic ticket receipts in $ millions)

	RECEIPTS	TITLE	YEAR OF RELEASE
1.	$601	Titanic	1997
2.	$461	Star Wars: Episode IV: A New Hope	1977
3.	$437	Shrek 2	2004
4.	$433	ET	1982
5.	$431	Star Wars: Episode I: The Phantom Menace	1999
6.	$407	Spider-Man	2002
7.	$377	The Lord of the Rings : Return of the King	2003
8.	$373	Spider-Man 2	2004
9.	$370	The Passion of the Christ	2004
10.	$357	Jurassic Park	1993
11.	$341	The Lord of the Rings: The Two Towers	2002
12.	$340	Finding Nemo	2003
13.	$329	Forrest Gump	1994
14.	$329	The Lion King	1994
15.	$318	Harry Potter and the Sorcerer's Stone	2001
16.	$314	The Lord of the Rings: The Fellowship of the Ring	2001
17.	$311	Star Wars: Episode II: Attack of the Clones	2002
18.	$309	Star Wars: Episode VI: The Return of the Jedi	1983
19.	$306	Independence Day	1996
20.	$305	Pirates of the Caribbean: The Curse of the Black Pearl	2003
21.	$294	The Sixth Sense	1999
22.	$290	Star Wars: Episode V: The Empire Strikes Back	1980
23.	$286	Home Alone	1990
24.	$281	The Matrix Reloaded	2003
25.	$268	Shrek	2001
26.	$262	Harry Potter and the Chamber of Secrets	2002
27.	$260	Dr. Seuss' How the Grinch Stole Christmas	2000
28.	$260	Jaws	1975
29.	$256	Monsters Inc.	2001
30.	$251	Batman	989
31.	$250	Men in Black	1997
32.	$249	Harry Potter and the Prisoner of Azkaban	2004

33.	$246	Toy Story 2	1999
34.	$243	Bruce Almighty	2003
35.	$242	Raiders of the Lost Ark	1981
36.	$242	Twister	1996
37.	$241	My Big Fat Greek Wedding	2002
38.	$239	Ghostbusters	1984
39.	$235	Beverly Hills Cop	1984
40.	$234	Cast Away	2000
41.	$233	The Exorcist	2000
42.	$229	The Lost World: Jurassic Park	1997
43.	$228	Signs	2002
44.	$226	Rush Hour 2	2001
45.	$219	Mrs. Doubtfire	1993
46.	$218	Ghost	1990
47.	$217	Aladdin	1992
48.	$216	Saving Private Ryan	1998
49.	$215	Mission: Impossible 2	2000
50.	$215	X2: X-Men United	2003
57.	$199	Gone With the Wind	1939
64.	$185	Snow White and the Seven Dwarfs	1937

The following are figures for the GDP deflator:

1937	13.5	1978	47.5	1986	80.6	1993	102.6	2000	117.6
1939	13.7	1980	60.4	1987	83.1	1994	105.0	2001	120.1
1965	25.0	1981	66.1	1988	86.1	1995	107.6	2002	121.9
1970	30.6	1982	70.2	1989	89.7	1996	109.7	2003	123.9
1973	35.4	1983	73.2	1990	93.6	1997	111.9	2004	125.5
1975	42.2	1984	75.9	1991	97.3	1998	114.8		
1977	47.5	1985	78.6	1992	100.0	1999	114.9		

Use the figures from the movie list and the GDP deflator to create a list of the top five highest grossing movies of all time in real dollars and compare it to the top five in nominal dollars.

Problem Set 8.10

The Misery Index

1. Take the data from Problem Sets 8.3 and 8.8 and fill in the following table.

	INFLATION	+ UNEMPLOYMENT	= MISERY INDEX		INFLATION	+ UNEMPLOYMENT	= MISERY INDEX
1960	1.7	5.5	7.2	1990	5.4	5.6	11.0
1961	1.0	6.7	7.7	1991	4.2	6.8	11.0
1962	1.0	5.5	6.5	1992	3.0	7.5	10.5
1963	1.3	5.7	7.0	1993	3.0	6.9	9.9
1964	1.3	5.2	6.5	1994	2.6	6.1	8.7
1965	1.6	4.5	6.1	1995	2.8	5.6	8.4
1966	2.9	3.8	6.7	1996	3.0	5.4	8.4
1967	3.1	3.8	6.9	1997	2.3	4.9	7.2
1968	4.2	3.6	7.8	1998	1.7	4.5	6.2
1969	5.5	3.5	9.0	1999	1.9	4.2	6.1
1970	5.7	4.9	10.6				
1971	4.4	5.9	10.3				
1972	3.2	5.6	8.8		To be provided by students		
1973	6.2	4.9	11.1				
1974	11.0	5.6	16.6	2000	_____	_____	_____
1975	9.1	8.5	17.6	2001	_____	_____	_____
1976	5.8	7.7	13.5	2002	_____	_____	_____
1977	6.5	7.1	13.6	2003	_____	_____	_____
1978	7.6	6.1	13.7	2004	_____	_____	_____
1979	11.3	5.8	17.1	2005	_____	_____	_____
1980	13.5	7.1	20.6				
1981	10.3	7.6	17.9	2006	_____	_____	_____
1982	6.2	9.7	15.9	2007	_____	_____	_____
1983	3.2	9.6	12.8				
1984	4.3	7.5	11.8	2008	_____	_____	_____
1985	3.6	7.2	10.8				
1986	1.9	7.0	8.9	2009	_____	_____	_____
1987	3.6	6.2	9.8				
1988	4.1	5.5	9.6	2010	_____	_____	_____
1989	4.8	5.3	10.1				

2. Using the Misery Index you calculated in Question 1 as a measure of economic well being, was there a period that you might consider "the good old days?" Was there a period that you might consider "the bad old days?"

3.   In what ways might the Misery Index be a valid measure of economic well being?

4.   In what ways might the Misery Index not be a valid measure of economic well being?

Problem Set 8.11

The Phillips Curve

Use the following historical data to plot the rate of inflation and the rate of unemployment in the problems that follow.

YEAR	INFLATION RATE	UNEMPLOYMENT RATE	YEAR	INFLATION RATE	UNEMPLOYMENT RATE
1960	1.4%	5.5%	1980	9.2%	7.1%
1961	1.2%	6.7%	1981	9.4%	7.6%
1962	1.3%	5.5%	1982	6.3%	9.7%
1963	1.2%	5.7%	1983	4.3%	9.6%
1964	1.5%	5.2%	1984	3.8%	7.5%
1965	2.0%	4.5%	1985	3.4%	7.2%
1966	2.8%	3.8%	1986	2.6%	7.0%
1967	3.2%	3.8%	1987	3.1%	6.2%
1968	4.3%	3.6%	1988	3.6%	5.5%
1969	4.7%	3.5%	1989	4.2%	5.3%
1970	5.3%	4.9%	1990	4.3%	5.6%
1971	5.2%	5.9%	1991	4.0%	6.8%
1972	4.2%	5.6%	1992	2.8%	7.5%
1973	5.6%	4.9%	1993	2.6%	6.9%
1974	9.0%	5.6%	1994	2.3%	6.1%
1975	9.4%	8.5%	1995	2.5%	5.6%
1976	5.8%	7.7%	1996	2.0%	5.4%
1977	6.5%	7.1%	1997	2.3%	4.9%
1978	7.3%	6.1%	1998	1.6%	4.5%
1979	8.5%	5.8%	1999	2.2%	4.2%

1. Plot the points for the decade of the 1960s on the graph below. Connect the points. Based on data and your line connecting the points, what conclusion might you come to about the relationship between unemployment and inflation for the decade of the 1960s?

2. What is this potential relationship called?

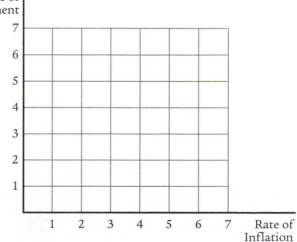

3. Repeat the process of question 1 for the decades of the 1970s, 1980s and 1990s.

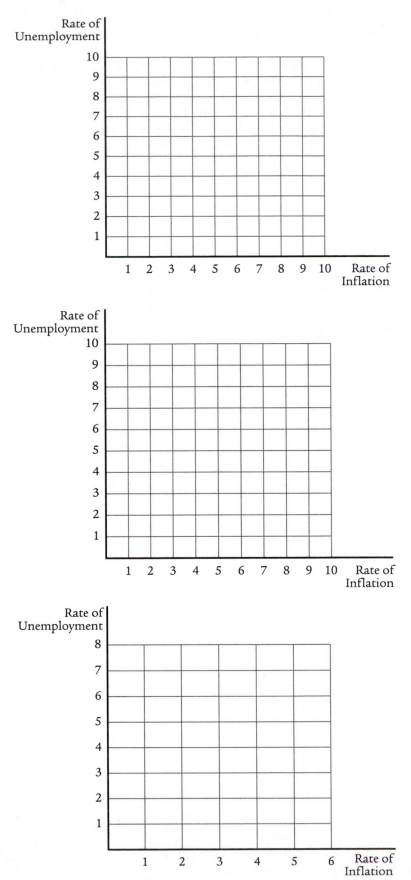

4. What can you conclude about this potential relationship over time?

5. Look up unemployment and inflation data and plot your own Phillips curve for the years from 2000 to the present.

Monetary and Fiscal Policy 9

Classroom Experiment 9.A

Anticipating Policy: Signs of the Times

Time Required: *30 minutes*	**Level of Difficulty:** *moderate to high.*
Materials Required: *recording tables provided*	**Textbook Coverage of Underlying Topics:** *Arnold Ch. 16, McConnell/Brue Ch. 15, Mankiw Ch. 34, Colander Ch. 28, McEachern Ch. 30, Baumol/Blinder Ch. 29*
Purpose: *To provide insight into the anticipating of policy and the policy ineffectiveness that results.*	

Introduction

Individuals and firms must make important decisions on the basis of incomplete signals about the economy. Firms make decisions about production and inventory levels. Individuals make decisions about labor contracts and consumption on the basis of accurate information about their own prices and wages but incomplete information about price and wage levels and trends for the rest of the nation. National information is reported on monthly or quarterly bases for those who seek it, but on any given day if the price of apples falls by 15 cents or our wage rises by 60 cents an hour, we face uncertainty about whether such changes represent deflation/inflation on a national scale or whether the changes only affect these selected goods and services. In other words, it is initially unclear whether these changes in *nominal* prices or wages (the actual dollar amounts) represent *real* changes (changes in what other goods we must forego to purchase an apple or in what we can buy with our wage). If all prices and wages are changing by the same proportion, there is no real effect. If the price of the things we buy and our income both double, our income will still buy the same amount of stuff. There is another source of possible uncertainty: The Federal Reserve or the government can swoop in and enact monetary or fiscal policy that changes the level of prices and wages. This experiment will give you a taste of the way people address each of these types of uncertainty and the implications on policy effectiveness.

Scenario

In this experiment you have entered a world in which the Fed is an unknown commodity. You do not initially know what type of strategy the Fed is following. They might follow a fixed-rule strategy that increases the money supply at the rate of GDP growth, they might adopt a more flexible strategy of discretionary monetary policy that responds to the condition of the economy with counter-cyclical measures, or they might just be out to lunch.

We'll use the price of an apple to indicate the price level for items that you purchase. Imagine that either you purchase only apples or that the prices of everything you purchase rise and fall with the price of apples. Let the symbol Pe represent your expectation of the price level for the current period, the true value of which you will not learn until the end of the day. Think of the real value of your wage as being the number of apples you can buy with it. Apples initially cost \$1 each and you earn a nominal wage of \$9 per hour—9 apples worth. If your wage stayed the same but the price of apples fell to 50 cents, your real wage (the purchasing power of the same \$9) would double, and you could purchase 18 apples for every hour of work.

Let S_L represent the number of hours you will work in a day. Suppose that your labor supply function is

$$S_L = \frac{\text{nominal wage}}{\text{expected price level}} = w/Pe.$$

Thus, each period you will work one hour for every apple you expect to be able to purchase with your real wage. Each morning you will get up, read the paper to see what's happening in the world, take a look at your nominal wage, and decide how many hours to work that day. Your labor supply decision will depend on your estimate of the price level. The trick is to decide whether observed changes in your nominal wage represent real changes as well. Your nominal wages may have increased or decreased by more than the general price level due to changes in the demand for the flamingo yard ornaments you produce. Alternatively, the general price level may have changed along with your wage due to Fed policy responses to the state of the economy, keeping your real wage (the number of apples you can purchase) unchanged. Do you feel somewhat in the dark? You should, but see what you can learn about the Fed's actions as you go along.

As you become aware of them, fill in the nominal wage (W), newspaper headline, your estimate of the price level (P_e), your labor supply ($S_L = W/P_e$), the actual price level for each period (P), and the real wage (Real $W = W/P$). As the game begins, the most recent price known for apples is \$1. Note that the headline refers to the economy at the end of the previous day. Any changes since then in the actual price are the result of Fed policy and not the news item.

PERIOD	W ($)	HEADLINE	P_e	S_L	ACTUAL P ($)	REAL W (APPLES)
1	_____	_____	_____	_____	_____	_____
2	_____	_____	_____	_____	_____	_____
3	_____	_____	_____	_____	_____	_____
4	_____	_____	_____	_____	_____	_____
5	_____	_____	_____	_____	_____	_____
6	_____	_____	_____	_____	_____	_____
7	_____	_____	_____	_____	_____	_____
8	_____	_____	_____	_____	_____	_____
9	_____	_____	_____	_____	_____	_____

Reflections

(Please answer these questions *after* completing the classroom experiment.)

1. How effective was the Fed's monetary policy in the beginning, middle, and end of this experiment?

2. What might the Fed need to do in order to make discretionary monetary policy effective?

3. Suppose the economy is at long-run equilibrium when the government tries to increase productivity and employment with expansionary monetary policy. Draw an ADAS diagram and label the equilibrium before expansionary monetary policy with an A, label the economy after expansionary monetary policy with a B, and label the equilibrium after workers and firms incorporate the price level increase into their wage and input-price contracts as C.

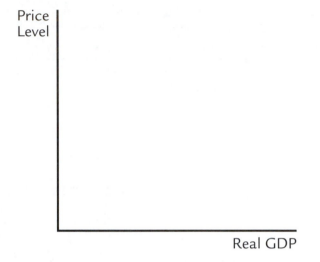

4. What is the relationship between the time it takes to move from point B to point C and the Fed's ability to reduce unemployment?

Afterthoughts

The efficacy of the Fed's actions depends on whether they are anticipated or not. If we know that the Fed always increases the money supply during a recession, we anticipate their behavior and build a price/wage increase into our expectations. The result is that we are not willing to work more hours at the higher nominal wage because we know that our real wage is unchanged. Our expectations render anticipated monetary policy ineffective. How effective is monetary policy in the real world? Ask four economists and you'll get five different opinions.

Denise Hazlett describes a similar activity called "The Lucas Island Experiment" in *Classroom Expernomics,* 5(2), (Fall 1996), at http://www.marietta.edu/~delemeeg/expernom/f96.html

Classroom Experiment 9.B

Outguessing the Fed (among others): Internet Stock Market Games

Time Required: *20 minutes at the beginning and end of the several-week period of the game*	**Level of Difficulty**: *low to moderate*
Materials Required: *Internet access*	**Textbook Coverage of Underlying Topics:** *Arnold Ch. 1, McConnell/Brue Ch. 1, Mankiw Ch. 1, Colander Ch. 1, McEachern Ch. 1, Baumol/Blinder Ch. 1*
Purpose: *To provide engagement in financial economics and exposure to the workings of the stock market.*	

Introduction

Financial markets bring those who want to save or take on risk together with those who want to borrow or reduce risk. The bond market and the stock market serve these purposes, as do financial intermediaries like banks. Perhaps the most exciting of these financial markets, the stock market, is also the most complex. It is difficult to grasp the rules and jargon of the stock market without being involved. Economists like John Maynard Keynes among others have made fortunes by predicting trends, policies, and market reactions to various events. Many others have lost fortunes with their guesswork, which makes the stock market expensive and risky—unless you're just pretending. That's what you can do in a virtual stock market game. The programming of an online stock market game is beyond the scope of this book, but we want to remind you of the possibilities and point you to some specific sites that provide good games at little or no charge.

Scenario

You or your instructor can choose from a variety of Internet stock market games. Three examples available at the time of this writing are:

- The Virtual Stock Exchange (http://www.virtualstockexchange.com/), which promotes a variety of competitions based on pretend trading of real stocks,

- The Stock Market Game™ (http://www.smg2000.org/), a program of the Securities Industry Foundation for Economic Education, an affiliate of the Securities Industry Association, and

- The Hollywood Stock Exchange (http://www.hsx.com/), in which you buy and sell shares of celebrities and productions in a virtual exchange.

Similar games often show up at colleges and online brokerages like Ameritrade.com. As an alternative, your instructor may simply ask everyone in the class to pick $50,000 worth of stocks today and then see whose stock portfolio increased in value by the largest percentage over a four week (+/−) period. There are also useful online descriptions of the myriad trading symbols and terms to complement this Internet activity. See, for example, Yahoo! Finance (http://finance.yahoo.com/), and the New York Stock Exchange Web site (http://www.nyse.com).

Reflections

(Please answer these questions *after* completing the classroom experiment.)

1. In what way is the stock market valuable to corporations?

2. In what way is the stock market valuable to investors?

3. As an investor, you bore some of the financial risks faced by the corporations whose shares you held. How did those risks play out, and how did you respond to those risks?

4. What strategy did you employ in your mock stock investing?

5. In an efficient market, the prices of the stocks should reflect all available information, meaning that opportunities for exceptional profit or loss occur only on a random basis. Why do you suppose some people consistently make large profits in the stock market, while others lose their shirts?

Afterthoughts

Financial markets are central to the success of our economy because they bring cash-strapped entrepreneurs together with cash-laden investors and risk takers together with those who want or need to avoid them. Futures markets serve a similar purpose, allowing farmers (for example) who can't afford the downside risk of price fluctuations to obtain a certain price for their unplanted crops by selling the rights to those forthcoming crops to speculators who think the price will go up. With humble beginnings such as Osaka's Dojima Rice Exchange in the 1730s, these markets are in many ways to thank for our current supply of food and commercial goods.

Problem Set 9.1

Fiscal Policy

1. Fill in the appropriate fiscal policy action in each square of the table, indicating the **direction** in which the policy tool above the square (government spending or taxation) should be changed to bring about the appropriate change in the problem to the left of the square (recession or inflation).

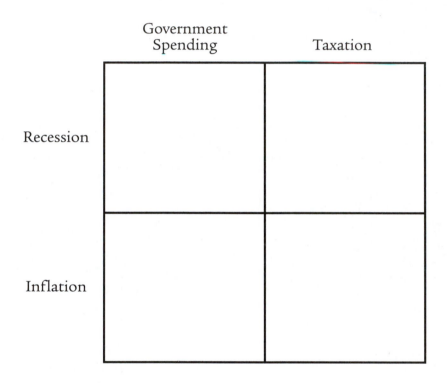

Problem Set 9.2

Monetary Policy

1. Fill in the appropriate monetary policy action in each square of the table, indicating the **direction** in which the policy tool above the square (open market operations, reserve requirements, or the discount rate) should be changed to bring about the appropriate change in the problem to the left of the square (recession or inflation).

	Open Market Operations	Reserve Requirements	Discount Rate
Recession			
Inflation			

Problem Set 9.3

Fiscal Policy and Monetary Policy

The federal government uses fiscal policy to act in a counter-cyclical manner. The Federal Reserve uses monetary policy for the same reason. Indicate the specific policy solution that would address the problems below within the given guidelines.

1. Monetary policy to correct for inflation, using the discount rate.

2. Fiscal policy to correct for inflation, using government spending.

3. Monetary policy to correct for inflation, using the reserve requirement.

4. Fiscal policy to correct for inflation, using tax changes.

5. Monetary policy to correct for inflation, using open market operations.

6. Monetary policy to correct for recession, using the discount rate.

7. Fiscal policy to correct for recession, using government spending.

8. Monetary policy to correct for recession, using the reserve requirement.

9. Fiscal policy to correct for recession, using tax changes.

10. Monetary policy to correct for recession, using open market operations.

Money and Banking 10

Classroom Experiment 10.A

Money Creation Experiment: Banks and Borrowers

Time Rrequired: *20–30 minutes*	**Level of Difficulty:** *low to moderate.*
Materials Required: *100 pennies or funny-money dollars*	**Textbook Coverage of Underlying Topics:** *Arnold Ch. 12, McConnell/Brue Ch. 14, Mankiw Ch. 29, Colander Ch. 27, McEachern Ch. 29, Baumol/Blinder Ch. 28*
Purpose: *To simulate the money-creation process and demystify this intricate reality.*	

Introduction

Money doesn't grow on trees, but believe it or not, it can be created almost out of thin air by the banking system. The U.S. has what is called a fractional reserve banking system in which only a fraction of total deposits is held on reserve in the banks' vaults and the rest is lent out. The ratio of a bank's reserves to a bank's deposits is called its reserve ratio, and the Fed sets a minimum reserve ratio for all banks. Deposits beyond the required reserves are called excess reserves and may be lent out. Banks earn profits by lending out their deposits at an interest rate a few percentage points higher than the rate they pay their depositors. In this experiment, you will be part of the money creation process and see how much money the banking system can "grow" out of a small initial deposit.

Scenario

As an individual, it isn't wise to hold much cash on hand because inflation erodes its value, not to mention the fact that it might get lost or stolen.

In this exercise, we will make the simplifying assumptions that individuals hold all of their money in banks and that banks loan out all of their excess reserves. Sitting in a semicircle (if possible), every other person will be a banker and the others will be borrowers. In real life, people borrow money from banks to spend it, and the businesspersons who receive that money from the spenders are likely to deposit it into their own banks. This experiment best exhibits money creation if we have as many banks and borrowers as possible, so we will cut out the businessperson role and assume that the borrower deposits the money directly into a bank account. Of course, for realism, we can think of this as the bank account of the businessperson from whom something was purchased.

Your instructor will deposit a dollar into the first bank (the first person in the semicircle) and announce the required reserve ratio. The first bank can then lend the excess reserves to the first borrower (the second person in the semicircle). The first borrower deposits all of these funds into the second bank (the third person in the circle), and so the process goes until there is no more money or no more people. Use the space below to record your holdings.

If you are a bank, indicate the amount of money you are holding as required reserves: _____

If you are a borrower, indicate the amount of money you have on deposit: _____

DEPOSIT (PENNIES)	REQUIRED RESERVES	LOAN
100	20	80
80	16	64
64	13	51
51	10	41
41	8	33
33	7	26
26	5	21
21	4	17
17	4	13
13	2	11
11	2	9
9	2	7
7	2	5
5	1	4
4	1	3
3	1	2
2	1	1
1	1	0
Total ≈ 500	Total = 100	Total ≈ 400

(Totals are approximate due to rounding.)

Reflections

(Please answer these questions *after* completing the classroom experiment.)

1. The required reserve ratio was _____. In the end, the total amount of money being held in banks was _____, and the total amount depositors had in their bank accounts was _____.

2. Economists claim that the money multiplier, equal to one divided by the required reserve ratio, tells us the total increase in the money supply created from each $1 in new deposits. Using the numbers from this experiment, check the veracity of the economists' assertion.

3. What would the total deposits have been after the money creation process in this experiment if the required reserve ratio had been 0.10? _____ How about if the required reserve ratio had been 0.50? _____

4. What do you suppose would happen if the initial depositor decided to withdraw her $1?

Afterthoughts

Your answers to question 3 indicate the sensitivity of the multiplier to the reserve requirement. In theory, modest changes in the required reserve ratio can result in large changes in the amount of money on deposit and, therefore, change the money supply. Money creation is indeed an important phenomenon in our economy, although open market operations and adjustments in the discount rate turn out to be more viable tools for monetary policy. One reason for this is that banks seldom loan out all of their excess reserves, making changes in the required reserve ratio relatively ineffectual. If we ever pay off our national debt, the Treasury will no longer need to borrow money by selling bonds, and the Fed will no longer be able to buy and sell those bonds on the open market to influence the money supply. That possibility makes money creation and alternative methods of influencing the money supply important topics.

Classroom Experiment 10.B

Barter vs. Money: Appreciating the Dollar

Time Required: *10–15 minutes*

Materials Required: *a chair, a pen, an eraser, a piece of chalk, and a lectern*

Purpose: *To demonstrate some of the virtues of money.*

Level of Difficulty: *low*

Textbook Coverage of Underlying Topics:
Arnold Ch. 14, McConnell/Brue Ch. 13, Mankiw Ch. 29, Colander Ch. 27, McEachern Ch. 28, Baumol/Blinder Ch. 28

Introduction

Money serves several valuable purposes in our economy. It provides a standard unit of account that makes price comparisons far easier than if backpacks cost 22 chickens at one location and 13 sacks of flour at another. It is a store of value that allows ski instructors to buy food in the summertime because they can convert their wintertime service into money that is readily storable until times of need. And it is a medium of exchange that frees us from having to barter for what we need. In a barter economy, those needing to purchase something hope for a *double coincidence of wants*, meaning that when two people get together to barter, each will want what the other has. Bartering is seldom facilitated by such luck. In this experiment, you will see what happens when it is not.

Scenario

This experiment is inspired by an episode of the old Korean War situation comedy *M*A*S*H,* in which the surgical unit needs penicillin, but the people who have penicillin don't want anything that the surgical unit has. This precipitates a series of bartered trades of what the unit does have for what other parties have ultimately to gain the penicillin. In the classroom experiment, someone who only has a chair to trade will seek out a pen. With chair in hand, the pen seeker will visit with the people on his or her street (row of desks) one at a time, starting with those closest to him or her, trying to barter for a pen by obtaining that which the pen owner desires. He or she can ask the neighbors what they have and what they would be willing to accept for their possessions. (Items cannot be appropriated from any other source.) As you watch or participate in this experiment, you will gain firsthand understanding of the complexity of life without money.

Reflections

(Please answer these questions *after* completing the classroom experiment.)

1. How would this experiment have been different if everyone had $100 in cash?

2. How often does the person who has what you want, want what you have, creating a double coincidence of wants?

3. Beyond the lack of double coincidences of wants, what other problems are presented by the need to barter?

4. In what settings might bartering be necessary because money is unavailable?

5. Some people see money as the root of evil. Would things be better if we didn't have money?

Afterthoughts

Money turns out to be a blessing, despite its reputation as a source of greed. The ease of exchange, value storage, and accounting using a standard form of money have led most civilizations to concoct some form of money, be it shells, arrowheads, carved stones, or precious metals. Perhaps in most societies, it was the refrigerator salesperson who was first to push for the adoption of a common currency. (Refrigerators are heck to carry around and barter with!)

Problem Set 10.1

Bank Expansion of Demand Deposits

In a fractional reserve banking system, an initial deposit in a bank can lead to a larger total bank expansion of the money supply. Assume that all banks can immediately loan out all of their excess reserves, that the reserve requirement is 20 percent of deposits, and that all excess reserves loaned out are deposited into another bank.

A stranger comes into Econville and deposits $2,000 into Bank 1.

1. How much will Bank 1 have to keep in reserve?

2. How much will Bank 1 be able to loan out as excess reserves?

3. How much will be deposited into Bank 2?

4. How much will Bank 2 have to keep in reserve?

5. How much will Bank 2 be able to loan out as excess reserves?

6. How much will be deposited into Bank 3?

7. How much will Bank 3 have to keep in reserve?

8. How much will Bank 3 be able to loan out as excess reserves?

9. How much will be deposited into Bank 4?

10. How much will Bank 4 have to keep in reserve?

11. How much will Bank 4 be able to loan out as excess reserves?

12. How much will be deposited into Bank 5?

13. How much will Bank 5 have to keep in reserve?

14. How much will Bank 5 be able to loan out as excess reserves?

15. If this process continues, what will eventually be the total expansion of the money supply?

16. How much of the money in question 15 was created by the banking system?

Problem Set 10.2

The Reserve Requirement and the Money Multiplier

The Central Bank sets the reserve requirement for the banking system of Econville. All banks in Econville must keep the required reserves on deposit at the Central Bank or in their vaults in the form of cash. All banks loan out their excess reserves.

A $10,000.00 deposit is made into a bank in Econville. For the following reserve requirements, fill in the amount of required reserves.

1.   10 percent

2.   20 percent

3.   25 percent

4.   33 1/3 percent

5.   50 percent

For each of the following reserve requirements fill in the amount of excess reserves.

6.   10 percent

7.   20 percent

8.   25 percent

9.   33 1/3 percent

10.   50 percent

The money multiplier is 1 divided by the reserve requirement. For each of the following reserve requirements, fill in the money multiplier.

11. 10 percent

12. 20 percent

13. 25 percent

14. 33 1/3 percent

15. 50 percent

The total amount by which the money supply can expand is the money multiplier times the amount of the initial deposit. For each of the following reserve requirements fill in the amount by which the money supply could expand.

16. 10 percent

17. 20 percent

18. 25 percent

19. 33 1/3 percent

20. 50 percent

Aggregate Supply, Aggregate Demand, and Aggregate Expenditure

11

Classroom Experiment 11.A

Getting into the (Circular) Flow of Things

Time Required: *15–20 minutes*	**Textbook Coverage of Underlying Topics:**
Materials Required: *inhibition*	*Arnold Ch. 5,* *McConnell/Brue Ch. 2,* *Mankiw Ch. 2, Colander Ch. 26,*
Purpose: *To reinforce understanding of the circular flow.*	*McEachern Ch. 22,* *Baumol/Blinder Ch. 24*
Level of Difficulty: *low to moderate.*	

Introduction

What goes around comes around. This universal truth is central to macroeconomics as well. The factors of production—land, labor, capital, and entrepreneurship—flow from households to firms through the factor market and then back to households in the form of goods and services via the product market. Dollars flow in the opposite direction, going from households to firms in exchange for goods and services via the product market, and then back to households in exchange for inputs via the factor market. We are all parts of this flow in one way or another. To follow the entire path within the course of a few minutes is to gain a fuller and more memorable perspective on the circular flow than most people are fortunate enough to experience.

Scenario

Okay, stop thinking about your lack of a date for Friday night because you're about to be a refrigerator. That's right. You read over the circular flow description, but it didn't soak in because you didn't pretend you were a refrigerator and ride the tide, so buck up and put on a chill. You and the rest of the class will tour the circular flow, taking the role of inputs, goods, or the money exchanged for them. To be more specific, you will represent the inputs that go into refrigerators, the refrigerators themselves, and then money on the return trip. Your instructor will designate the four corners of your room as households, factor markets, firms, and product markets respectively. Starting at home in the household corner, the class will shuffle through the factor markets to the firms as labor, steel, plastic, and coolant. The firms transform these inputs into refrigerators (representing all goods and services), and you will shuffle as a fridge from the firms through the product markets to the households. After arriving in a household kitchen, you will change form and direction and head to the product markets as money. The expenditure on refrigerators in the product markets goes to the firms, where you take a right turn and the money goes to the factor market as payment for the inputs that went into production. Think about what you are as you move from one place to another. Once you've made it around in both directions, try it once more for good measure.

Reflections

(Please answer these questions *after* completing the classroom experiment.)

1. In what sense can we say that "what goes around comes around" in this context?

2. What are some of the complexities of the real-world circular flow that are left out of this simple model?

3. What would happen if there were a significant snag in one section of the circular flow? For example, what if an energy crisis prevented refrigerators from being delivered from the product markets to the households?

4. What does it mean when people say that "firms don't pay taxes, people do"?

Afterthoughts

Are you dizzy? Thanks for going along for the ride. It's important to know how the various sectors of our economy fit together and feed into each other. When you're asked to recount the journey of the circular flow on the exam, it will be nice to know that you've been there and done that.

Classroom Experiment 11.B

Experimenting with the Marginal Propensity to Consume: Easy Come, Easy Go

---

Time Required: *10–15 minutes*

Materials Required: *none*

Purpose: *To allow players to generate and work with their own consumption and savings functions, and, thereby, clarify the meaning and importance of these functions.*

Level of Difficulty: *moderate. Mistakes are often made by those who don't take their time.*

Textbook Coverage of Underlying Topics:
Arnold Ch. 9,
McConnell/Brue Ch. 9,
Mankiw (not covered),
Colander Ch. 26,
McEachern Ch. 24,
Baumol/Blinder Ch. 24

Introduction

With increasing incomes come the joys and trials of deciding what to do with the new money. In the *Balancing Act* experiment, you were asked to allocate the budget of the federal government. Allocating personal budgets is another ballgame entirely. The fact that you're smart enough to take economics is a good indication that you yourself are upwardly mobile and will see large increases in your weekly income over the next few decades. For the purposes of this experiment, we would like to speed that process up a little bit. Have fun and spend wisely.

Scenario

As this experiment begins, you are strapped for cash. Can you relate? Your income is zero, and you must borrow to pay for the essentials. Then you will swiftly receive the career of your dreams and be asked to consider how your consumption and savings levels would be affected by a series of alternative income levels. At each income level, assume that you do not foresee another raise in the near future, that the income described is net of taxes and transfers, and that all of your money must be allocated among the following spending and savings categories:

Housing This includes your rent or mortgage payment, furniture, utilities, repairs, and so on.

Transportation Travel, commuting, auto insurance and repairs, gasoline, . . .

Entertainment Sports, recreation, concert tickets, computers, books, music, . . .

Health Food, medical care, dental care, eyeglasses, toiletries, . . .

Other Clothing, gifts, childcare, . . .

Savings/Debt Repayment Dollars placed here go to pay off any existing loans, and then accumulate as savings.

Imagine that you are presently unemployed and have no savings or other forms of wealth. You must borrow to make all of your purchases. In the left column of blanks below, fill in the minimum amount you could spend on each of these categories. Since your consumption is initially financed by debt, your total consumption expenditure will equal your debt in the first column. To distinguish your debt amount from savings, place a negative sign in front of values that represent debt.

In the following columns, please indicate the *additional* amount of money you would spend on each category if, instead of earning the previous income, your income were increased by $100 to the level indicated. For example, with the second $100 increase, your total weekly income would be $200. If you would spend $30 more per week on housing than you would with a $100 weekly income, write "30" on the line below "200" and across from Housing. The total of your additional expenditure on all consumption and savings should equal the amount of your raise—$100— in each of the last five columns. Remember that at each income level, you are to imagine that you do not foresee any subsequent pay raise.

Raise ($)		+100	+100	+100	+100	+100
Total Weekly Income ($)	0	100	200	300	400	500

MINIMUM EXPENDITURE: PORTION OF *ADDITIONAL* $100 SPENT ON:

Housing   _____ _____ _____ _____ _____ _____

Transportation _____ _____ _____ _____ _____ _____

Entertainment   _____ _____ _____ _____ _____ _____

MINIMUM EXPENDITURE: PORTION OF *ADDITIONAL* $100 SPENT ON:

Health   _____ _____ _____ _____ _____ _____

Other   _____ _____ _____ _____ _____ _____

All Consumption _____ _____ _____ _____ _____ _____

Savings/Debt _____ _____ _____ _____ _____ _____

Reflections

(Please answer these questions *after* completing the classroom experiment.)

1. Your marginal propensity to consume (MPC) is the fraction of additional dollars of disposable income that is spent on consumption. Your marginal propensity to save (MPS) is the fraction of additional dollars of disposable income that is devoted to savings/debt repayment. You can determine your MPC at each income level by dividing the additional expenditure on consumption by the amount of the addition to income—$100. You can calculate MPS either as 1 – MPC or by dividing the additional savings at a particular income level by the additional $100 in income. Please fill in the following table:

Total Weekly Income ($)	100	200	300	400	500
MPC	_____	_____	_____	_____	_____
MPS	_____	_____	_____	_____	_____

2. The data you have generated above also permits you to observe your marginal propensity to consume within each of the categories listed. Look at how your additional spending on each item varied as your income increased from 0 to $500 per week.

   a. Which item(s) had a generally increasing MPC?

   b. Which item(s) had a generally decreasing MPC?

   c. Which item(s) had a generally constant MPC?

   d. Do the answers above fit in with what you have learned about economic theory as it applies to luxuries and necessities?

3. Calculate the net savings and total consumption expenditure at each income level. To find the net savings, simply add up the initial debt (as a negative number) and the dollars devoted to savings/debt repayment out of each raise leading up to the income level you are working on. For example, to find the total devoted to savings/debt at the $300 income level, add up the initial debt and the dollars devoted to savings/debt out of the first three $100 raises. The total consumption expenditure is calculated similarly, by adding up the zero-income consumption and the additional consumption at each income level up to the one you are working on.

Total Weekly Income ($)	0	100	200	300	400	500
Total for Savings/Debt	____	____	____	____	____	____
Total Consumption	____	____	____	____	____	____

4. Graph your total savings/debt and total consumption on the same graph, with real disposable income on the horizontal axis and real consumption expenditures on the vertical axis. (The designation as "real" means that we are measuring the purchasing power of dollars rather than simply the number of dollars. If the dollar values of our income and all prices doubled, there would be no real effect because we could still buy the same amount of everything with our income.)

5. How would you expect the consumption line to shift in the following situations?

   a. You win $10,000 in the lottery.

   b. You foresee a large recession and the likelihood of unemployment in the near future.

   c. Price levels fall.

Afterthoughts

The consumption function and marginal propensity to consume that you have studied here are important in part because they are the basis for the upward-sloping nature of the aggregate expenditure function that you will encounter soon. In simple models, MPC is the slope of both the consumption function *and* the aggregate expenditure function. Of further importance, *MPS* = 1 – *MPC* and 1/*MPS* is the spending multiplier, which tells us the total increase in real GDP resulting from each new dollar of autonomous spending (spending that does not depend on income, such as government spending). Now that you've generated and worked with consumption and savings functions yourself, the applications of these values should make more sense.

Jurgen Brauer describes a similar experiment in "A Savings/Consumption Game for Introductory Macroeconomics," *Classroom Expernomics*, 3(2) (Fall 1994), http://www.marietta.edu/~delemeeg/expernom/f94.html. Brauer updates this experiment in "A Savings/Consumption Game: An Update," *Classroom Expernomics*, 7(1) (Spring 1998), http://www.marietta.edu/~delemeeg/expernom/s98.html.

Problem Set 11.1

Monetary Policy and the Aggregate Supply/Aggregate Demand Model

Complete the following graphs to demonstrate the transmission mechanism of monetary policy.

1. Lowering the reserve requirement.

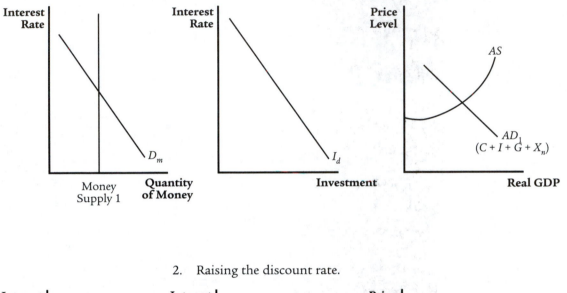

2. Raising the discount rate.

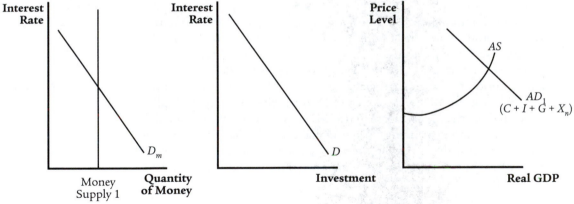

3. Selling bonds on the open market.

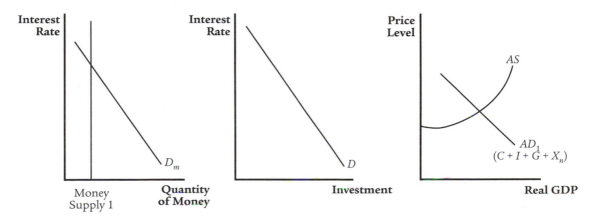

4. Raising the reserve requirement.

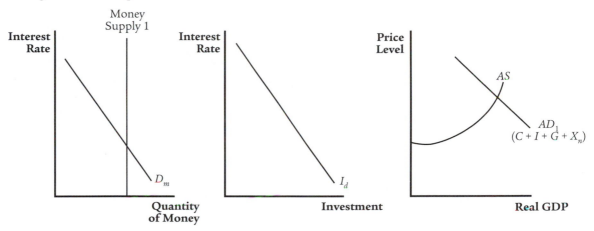

5. Lowering the discount rate.

6.   Buying bonds on the open market.

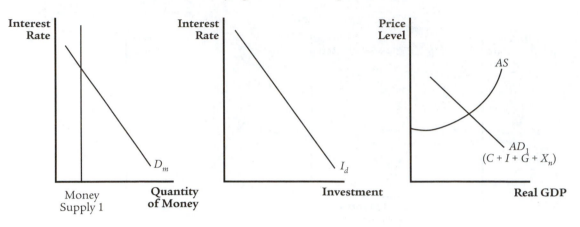

Problem Set 11.2

Monetary Policy and the Aggregate Expenditure Model

Complete the following graphs to demonstrate the transmission mechanism of monetary policy.

1. Lowering the reserve requirement.

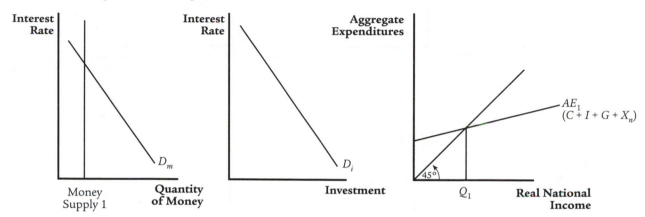

2. Raising the discount rate.

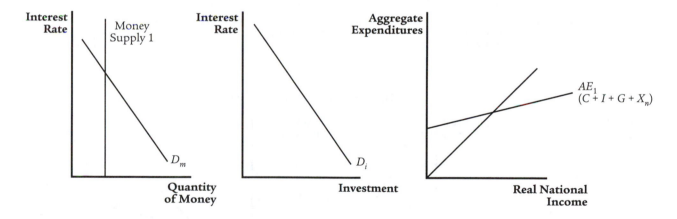

3. Selling bonds in the open market.

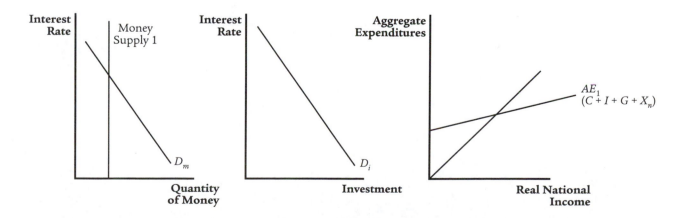

4.   Raising the reserve requirement.

5.   Lowering the discount rate.

6.   Buying bonds in the open market.

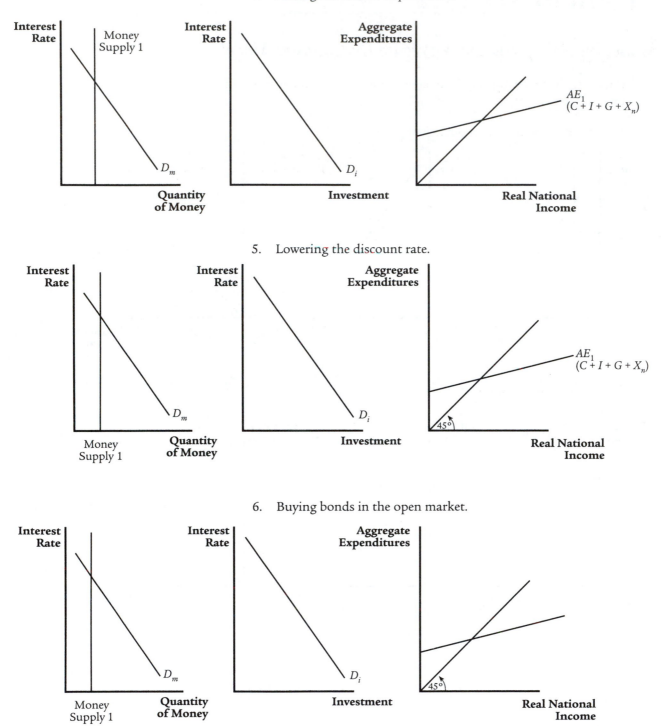

Problem Set 11.3

The Aggregate Expenditure Model

Answer the following questions based on the information in the graph below.

1. What is the level of investment spending?

2. What is the level of government spending?

3. What is the equilibrium level of real national income?

4. Calculate the marginal propensity to consume.

5. Assuming that savings is the only type of leakage, calculate the marginal propensity to save.

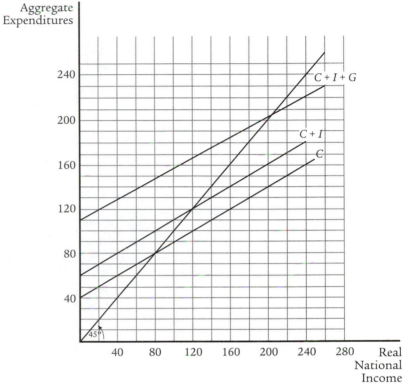

6. Calculate the simple multiplier.

7. If full employment would be reached with a real national income level of 250, what type of gap presently exists in this economy?

8. Should government spending increase or decrease to correct the situation you identified in question 7? By how much?

9. Should taxes be increased or decreased to correct the situation you identified in question 7? By how much?

Problem Set 11.4

Aggregate Supply and Aggregate Demand

Use an aggregate supply and aggregate demand diagram like the one shown below to demonstrate the effect of each of the following. In each case make only one shift, in either aggregate supply or aggregate demand. Example: The government decreases spending and increases taxes.

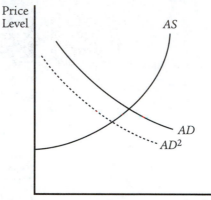

1.   Consumer confidence grows for the third straight month.

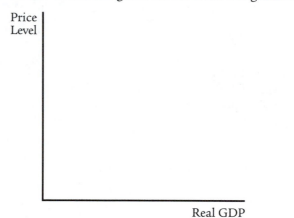

2.   A technological breakthrough lowers the cost of energy.

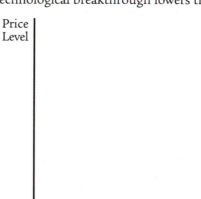

3. The government engages in a new highway construction program.

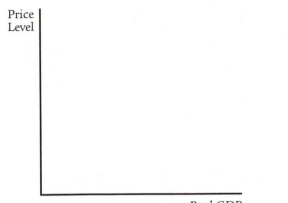

4. A series of natural disasters disrupts the production and delivery of goods.

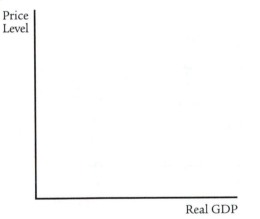

5. Laws are tightened to make immigration more difficult and this leads to labor shortages.

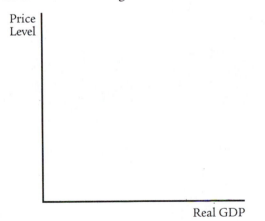

6. Interest rates fall.

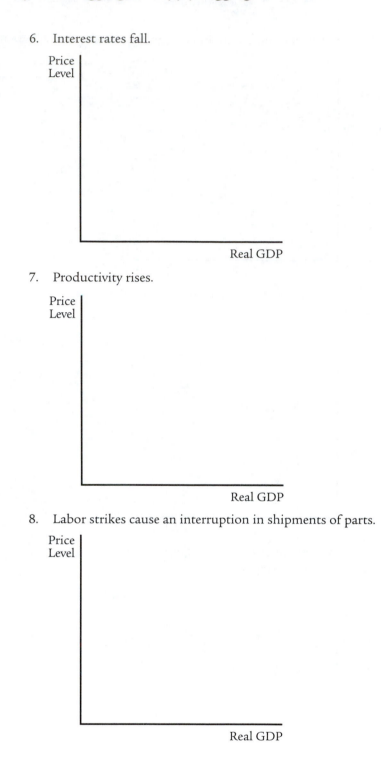

Price Level

Real GDP

7. Productivity rises.

Price Level

Real GDP

8. Labor strikes cause an interruption in shipments of parts.

Price Level

Real GDP

9. Increased graduation rates for schools lead to a more-skilled work-
force.

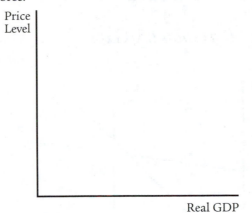

10. Stock and bond markets soar.

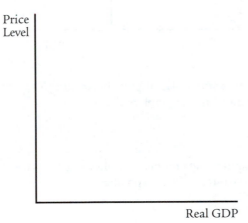

Problem Set 11.5

Inflationary and Recessionary Gaps

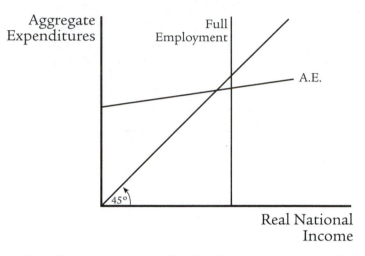

1. Describe an appropriate fiscal policy measure to remedy the situation demonstrated in the graph above.

2. Describe an appropriate monetary policy measure to remedy the situation demonstrated in the graph above.

3. Describe an appropriate fiscal policy measure to remedy the situation demonstrated in the graph below.

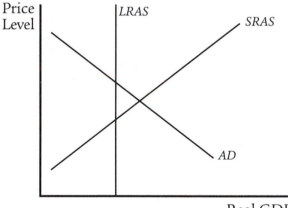

4. Describe an appropriate monetary policy measure to remedy the situation demonstrated in the graph below.

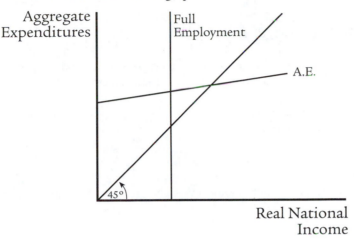

5. Describe an appropriate fiscal policy measure to remedy the situation demonstrated in the graph above.

6. Describe an appropriate monetary policy measure to remedy the situation demonstrated in the graph above.

7. Describe an appropriate fiscal policy measure to remedy the situation demonstrated in the graph below.

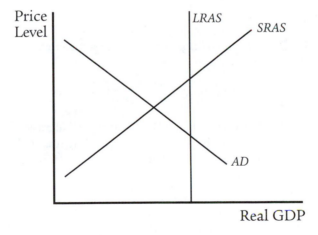

8. Describe an appropriate correct monetary policy measure to remedy the situation demonstrated in the graph above.

Problem Set 11.6

Balanced Budget Multiplier

In Econville, the marginal propensity to consume is 0.80 and the equilibrium level of real GDP is $300 less than full employment output.

1. Quantify the appropriate change in government spending to correct the situation.

2. By how much should taxes change to correct this situation using taxes?

3. If this economy had a law requiring a balanced government budget every year, meaning that government spending was tied to government revenues, could the situation be corrected? How?

Suppose that the situation in the economy described above changes so that now it is operating at a GDP level that is $100 more than the full employment level of GDP.

4. Quantify the appropriate change in government spending to correct the situation?

5. By how much should taxes change to correct this situation using taxes?

6. If this economy had a law requiring a balanced government budget every year so that government spending was tied to government revenues, could the situation be corrected? How?

International Economics

12

Classroom Experiment 12.A

The Benefits from Trade: Utility Gains from a Lunch Sack

<table>
<tr><td>Time Required: 10–15 minutes</td><td>Level of Difficulty: low</td></tr>
<tr><td>Materials Required: Each person needs one or more random knickknacks worth about 25 cents (lunch sack optional).</td><td rowspan="2">Textbook Coverage of Underlying Concepts:
Arnold Ch. 32,
McConnell/Brue Ch. 36,
Mankiw Ch. 9, Colander Ch. 21,
McEachern Ch. 19,
Baumol/Blinder Ch. 33</td></tr>
<tr><td>Purpose: To demonstrate the gains from trade</td></tr>
</table>

Introduction

Our global community struggles with issues of international trade and how open it should be, but certain aspects of trade should be clear. This experiment illuminates the potential benefits of trade. Iraq has oil, the United States has fields of wheat, and Columbia produces excellent coffee. The act of bringing these varied goods to the trading table provides opportunities for increased satisfaction for every country involved. Mutually beneficial trades draw on our comparative advantages and cater to our differing preferences. In this experiment, we feel those benefits firsthand.

Scenario

Your instructor will either supply or ask you to bring in one or more knick-knacks, "white elephants," or other tradable items. You will have the opportunity to conduct trades with classmates during a five-minute trading period. First, let's gauge your degree of happiness.

Given your current state of affairs and possessions, including the knickknack you obtained for this experiment, how happy are you on a scale of 1 to 100? A rating of one means that you are utterly and completely unhappy, a rating of 50 means that you are feeling so-so, and a rating of 100 means that you are in eternal bliss. What's your number?

_____

Your classroom is your microcosm of the world. When the trading period begins, take your tradable item(s) around the classroom and see if you can make one or more trades to acquire items that you prefer over your own.

Reflections

(Please complete these *after* the trading period has ended.)

1. On a scale of 1 to 100, how happy are you now that the trading period is over?

2. When your instructor surveyed the class to see how many were happier after trading than before, roughly what proportion of your class reported that they were happier?

3. Why is it unlikely that anyone was made worse off as the result of the trading period?

4. Explain how an improvement in the overall utility level of your class was achieved without bringing any additional resources into the classroom.

5. What implications do these findings have on the advisability of trade? What drawbacks from trade must be considered when formulating trade policy?

Afterthoughts

My elementary school had no cafeteria. I would bring a sack lunch each day and spend the first five minutes of the lunch period trading what I had for what others had. My house had an abundance of canned fruit and Halloween candy, whereas my friends had sandwiches that I wasn't good at making and other foods not available in my home. It was not difficult to find mutually beneficial trades. The experiment above, like lunchroom food bartering, provides a simple-yet-striking example of the gains from trade. The message is not that free trade is always good, but that we must not neglect its potential to make things better for everyone involved.

Classroom Experiment 12.B

Comparative Advantage Experiment: To Everyone's Advantage

Time Required: *20–30 minutes*	**Level of Difficulty:** *moderate. Players are asked to negotiate terms of trade, which isn't always easy.*
Materials Required: *none*	
Purpose: *To provide first-hand knowledge of the conditions under which mutually advantageous trade is possible, and to reinforce understanding of the concepts of comparative and absolute advantage.*	**Textbook Coverage of Underlying Topics:** *Arnold Ch. 32, McConnell/Brue Ch. 36, Mankiw Ch. 9, Colander Ch. 21, McEachern Ch. 19, Baumol/Blinder Ch. 33*

Introduction

There is heated disagreement among policymakers regarding the opportunity to benefit from trade. Protectionists worry that poorer countries can't provide real benefits to richer countries, and that for a rich country to trade with a poor country is tantamount to giving the poor country charity money. Advocates of free trade argue that two countries can benefit from trade as long as the relative costs of producing goods differ between the countries.

Economists say a country has a **comparative advantage** over another country in the production of a good if, in order to make each unit of the good, it foregoes less in terms of the production of other goods than the other country. In other words, it has a lower "opportunity cost" of producing the good. A country has an **absolute advantage** over another country in the production of a good if it can make that good using fewer inputs per unit of output than the other country. If the two countries have identical resources and both countries devote their resources to the production of the same good, the country with the absolute advantage would be able to produce more of the good than the country with the absolute disadvantage.

Scenario

Consider yourself a dictator in charge of trade for a country. (Your instructor will tell you which country you represent and with which country you are trading.) The graphs on the next page represent the production possibilities for each of the countries. For example, using all of its resources, in one period (let's call it a day), country A could produce 40 cars if it devoted all of its resources to car production, 40 computers if it devoted all of its resources to computers, or any of the combinations of cars and computers represented by points on the production possibilities frontier. It cannot make both 40 cars and 40 computers, for example, because each point on the line is only possible using *all* of the country's resources. As you learned in the links and smiles experiment, or will learn soon enough in your class, it is a simplification to have these lines straight rather than curved.

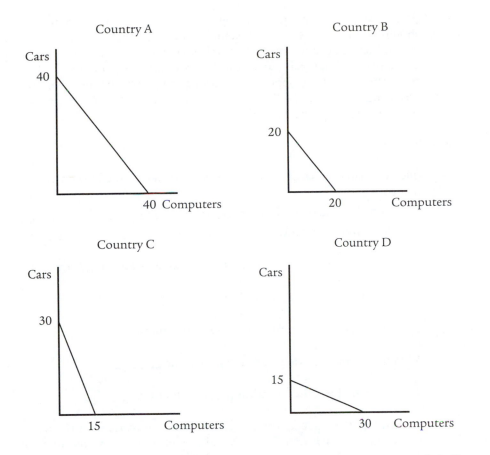

Assume that in the absence of trade, your country chooses to make exactly half of its maximum capacity of both goods. That is, the midpoint on the production possibilities frontier is the most favorable point for you. You are to negotiate with the representative of the country you are paired with to see if you can establish terms of trade—an exchange of some quantity of goods that you produce for some quantity of goods that the other country produces—that provide both countries with more of both goods than without trade. If you come to an agreement, write down the number of cars per computer in your exchange and the total number of cars and computers that changed hands. You will have 10 minutes to complete this negotiation. There are three questions you should consider before you begin your negotiations:

1. What is your opportunity cost for making each car? ＿＿＿

2. What is your opportunity cost for making each computer? ＿＿＿

3. What is the range of trade prices, in cars per computer, that would benefit your country **and** the country you are negotiating with?

(Hint: Calculate each country's opportunity cost of computers. If trade should occur, it is wise for each country to export what it has a comparative advantage in and import what it has a comparative disadvantage in. The mutually beneficial range of trade prices [in cars per computer] are those that exceed the opportunity cost of computers for the computer-exporting country and fall below the opportunity cost of computers for the computer-importing country.)

Reflections

(Please answer these questions *after* completing the classroom experiment.)

Which country did you represent? _____

Which country did you negotiate with? _____

Between your country and the country you were negotiating with:

1. Which had a comparative advantage in cars? _____

2. Which had a comparative advantage in computers? _____

3. Which had an absolute advantage in cars? _____

4. Which had an absolute advantage in computers? _____

5. Explain the trade agreement, if any, that you made with the representative you were paired with and why both parties were willing to participate in this trade.

6. Beyond international trade, list two other situations in which comparative advantages might lead to benefits from specialization and exchange.

7. On the graph below, draw the production possibilities frontier for your country. Indicate with an "X" the point that represents the number of cars and computers that your country will *produce* after trade. Then indicate with a big dot the point that represents the number of cars and computers that your country can *consume* per period after your trade.

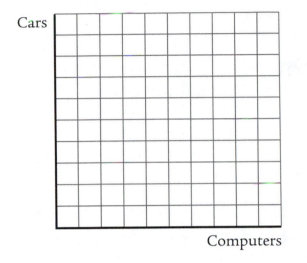

Cars

Computers

8. Are there any two countries that would not be able to form a mutually beneficial trade agreement? Explain.

Afterthoughts

Now you can probably guess where economists generally stand on the debate over free trade. Impediments to free trade such as tariffs, quotas, and other protectionist policies prevent the mutual gains available whenever one country has a comparative advantage over another. If you're thinking it's time to get more economists in Congress, we're with you!

Problem Set 12.1

Exchange Rates

Currency markets establish the international value of a nation's monetary unit. The exchange rate determined in these markets is a function of the supply of, and the demand for, these various currencies. The following table lists fictional exchange rates for selected countries.

Table 1

EXCHANGE RATE

France (euro)	.80	equals U.S.	$1.00
Canada (dollar)	1.40	equals U.S.	$1.00
Japan (yen)	150.00	equals U.S.	$1.00
Britain (pound)	.50	equals U.S.	$1.00

Using the values in the table above, calculate the following:

1. A $150.00 hotel room in the United States would cost a Japanese tourist _____ yen.

2. A $30,000.00 American car would cost a Canadian citizen _____ Canadian dollars.

3. A $15.00 compact disc from the U.S. would cost a person from France _____ euros.

4. A $5,000.00 Canadian dollar fly-in fishing trip would cost an American _____ U.S. dollars.

5. A $2,000.00 weekend at Disney World in Orlando, Florida would cost someone from England _____ British pounds.

Answer the following questions using the assumption that the values in Table 1 have changed to those shown in Table 2.

Table 2

EXCHANGE RATE

France (euro)	0.80	equals U.S.	$2.00
Canada (dollar)	1.40	equals U.S.	$2.00
Japan (yen)	150.00	equals U.S.	$2.00
Britain (pound)	.50	equals U.S.	$2.00

6. American-made goods would become relatively _____ to citizens of other countries.

7. Foreign-made goods in America would become relatively _____.

8. The price of domestically made goods in America would _____.

9. American exports would _____.

10. American imports would _____.

11. The U.S. dollar has _____ from the values shown in Table 1 to those shown in Table 2.

Problem Set 12.2

Contractionary Fiscal Policy, Interest Rates, and Net Exports

Please fill in the blanks and answer the questions that follow:

The government of Econville could engage in contractionary fiscal policy by either _____ government spending or _____ taxes.

1. On the graph below, demonstrate the effect of contractionary fiscal policy.

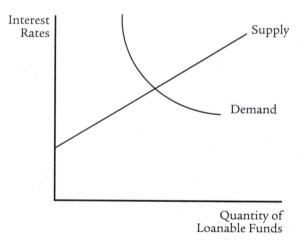

2. The change in the graph results in a/an _____ in interest rates in Econville.

3. How would the change in interest rates identified in question 2 affect business spending (Investment)?

4. Would this change in business spending support or counteract the original purpose the government of Econville had in mind?

5. On the graph below, demonstrate the effect of citizens of other countries observing the change in interest rates identified in question 2.

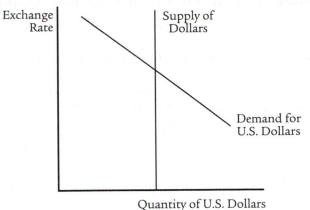

6. The change shown in the above graph would cause a/an _____ in the value of Econville currency.

7. As a result of this change in the value of Econville currency, exports would _____ .

8. As a result of this change in the value of Econville currency, imports would _____

9. Do the export effect and the import effect shown in questions 7 and 8 support or counteract the original purpose the government of Econville had in mind?

10. What is the economic term used to describe the effect discussed in question 3?

11. What is the economic term for the effect discussed in questions 7 and 8?

12. Use what you have learned in this problem to evaluate the effectiveness of contractionary fiscal policy.

Problem Set 12.3

Expansionary Fiscal Policy, Interest Rates, and Net Exports

Please fill in the blanks and answer the questions that follow:

The government of Econville could engage in expansionary fiscal policy by either _____ government spending or _____ taxes.

1. On the graph below, demonstrate the effect of expansionary fiscal policy.

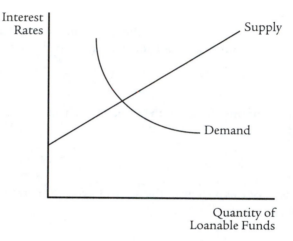

2. The changes in the graph above correspond with a/an _____ in interest rates in Econville.

3. How would the interest rate change identified in question 2 affect business spending (Investment)?

4. Would this change in business spending support or counteract the original purpose the government of Econville had in mind?

5. On the graph below, demonstrate the effect of citizens of other countries observing the change in interest rates identified in question 2.

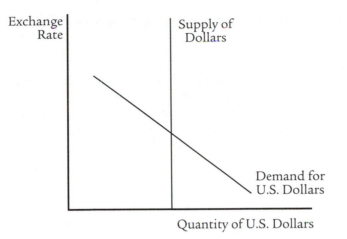

Quantity of U.S. Dollars

6. The change in the above graph would cause a/an _____ in the value of the currency of Econville.

7. As a result of this change in the currency value, Econville exports would _____.

8. As a result of this change in the currency value, Econville imports would _____.

9. Do the export effect and the import effect shown in questions 7 and 8 support or counteract the original purpose the government of Econville had in mind?

10. What is the economic term used to describe the effect discussed in question 3?

11. What is the economic term used to describe the effect discussed in questions 7 and 8?

12. What can you conclude about the effectiveness of expansionary fiscal policy?

Problem Set 12.4

Contractionary Monetary Policy, Interest Rates, and Net Exports

Please fill in the blanks and answer the questions that follow:

The Central Bank of Econville can engage in contractionary monetary policy by _____ the reserve requirement, _____ the discount rate, or _____ bonds.

1. On the graph below, demonstrate the effect of contractionary monetary policy by the Central Bank of Econville.

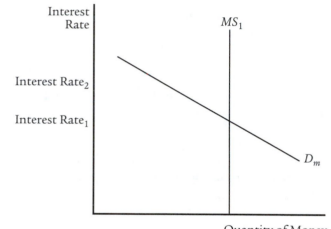

2. The changes in the above graph correspond with a/an _____ in interest rates in Econville.

3. How would the interest rate change from question 2 impact business spending (Investment)?

4. Would this change in business spending support or counteract the original purpose the Central Bank of Econville had in mind?

5. On the graph below, demonstrate the effect of citizens of other countries observing the change in interest rates shown in question 2.

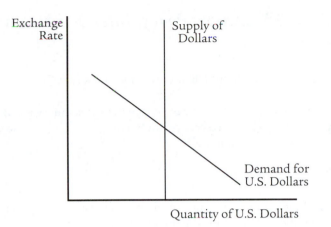

6. The change shown in the above graph would cause a/an _____ in the value of Econville currency.

7. As a result of this change in the currency value, Econville exports would _____ .

8. As a result of this change in the currency value, Econville imports would _____ .

9. Do the export effect and the import effect discussed in questions 7 and 8 support or counteract the original purpose the Central Bank of Econville had in mind?

10. What can you conclude about the effectiveness of contractionary monetary policy?

Problem Set 12.5

Expansionary Monetary Policy, Interest Rates, and Net Exports

Please fill in the blanks and answer the questions that follow:

The Central Bank of Econville can engage in expansionary monetary policy by _____ the reserve requirement, _____ the discount rate, or _____ bonds.

1. On the graph below demonstrate the effect of expansionary monetary policy by the Central Bank of Econville.

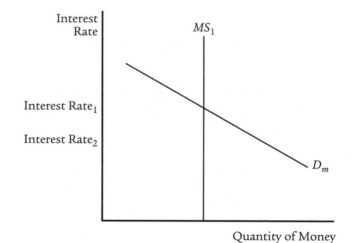

2. The changes in the above graph correspond with a/an _____ in interest rates in Econville.

3. How would the interest rate change from question 2 impact business spending (Investment)?

4. Would this change in business spending support or counteract the original purpose the Central Bank of Econville had in mind?

5. On the graph below, demonstrate the effect of citizens of other countries observing the change in interest rates shown in question 2.

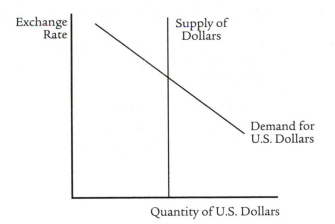

6. The change shown in the above graph would cause a/an _____ in the value of Econville currency.

7. As a result of this change in the currency value, Econville exports would _____.

8. As a result of this change in the currency value, Econville imports would _____ .

9. Do the export effect and the import effect discussed in questions 7 and 8 support or counter-act the original purpose the Central Bank of Econville had in mind?

10. What can you conclude about the effectiveness of expansionary monetary policy?

Problem Set 12.6

Comparative and Absolute Advantage

The countries of Karenville and Laurenland are able to produce root beer and pretzels. The following figures represent the output that can be produced with a fixed amount of factor inputs.

	KARENVILLE	LAURENLAND
Root beer	10	12
Pretzels	20	30

Answer the following questions on the basis of the information above.

1. Which country has an absolute advantage in the production of root beer? Explain how you arrived at your answer.

2. Which country has an absolute advantage in the production of pretzels? Explain how you arrived at your answer.

3. Which country has a comparative advantage in the production of root beer? Explain how you arrived at your answer.

4. Which country has a comparative advantage in the production of pretzels? Explain how you arrived at your answer.